NMAP
NETWORK SCANNING SERIES

NETWORK SECURITY, MONITORING, AND SCANNING LIBRARY

4 BOOKS IN 1

BOOK 1
NMAP FOR BEGINNERS: A PRACTICAL GUIDE TO NETWORK SCANNING

BOOK 2
NMAP MASTERY: ADVANCED TECHNIQUES AND STRATEGIES FOR NETWORK ANALYSIS

BOOK 3
NMAP SECURITY ESSENTIALS: PROTECTING NETWORKS WITH EXPERT SKILLS

BOOK 4
NMAP BEYOND BOUNDARIES: MASTERING COMPLEX NETWORK RECONNAISSANCE

ROB BOTWRIGHT

Published by Rob Botwright
Library of Congress Cataloging-in-Publication Data
ISBN 978-1-83938-653-4
Cover design by Rizzo

Disclaimer

The contents of this book are based on extensive research and the best available historical sources. However, the author and publisher make no claims, promises, or guarantees about the accuracy, completeness, or adequacy of the information contained herein. The information in this book is provided on an "as is" basis, and the author and publisher disclaim any and all liability for any errors, omissions, or inaccuracies in the information or for any actions taken in reliance on such information. The opinions and views expressed in this book are those of the author and do not necessarily reflect the official policy or position of any organization or individual mentioned in this book. Any reference to specific people, places, or events is intended only to provide historical context and is not intended to defame or malign any group, individual, or entity. The information in this book is intended for educational and entertainment purposes only. It is not intended to be a substitute for professional advice or judgment. Readers are encouraged to conduct their own research and to seek professional advice where appropriate. Every effort has been made to obtain necessary permissions and acknowledgments for all images and other copyrighted material used in this book. Any errors or omissions in this regard are unintentional, and the author and publisher will correct them in future editions.

BOOK 1: NMAP FOR BEGINNERS: A PRACTICAL GUIDE TO NETWORK SCANNING

BOOK 2: NMAP MASTERY: ADVANCED TECHNIQUES AND STRATEGIES FOR NETWORK ANALYSIS

BOOK 3: NMAP SECURITY ESSENTIALS: PROTECTING NETWORKS WITH EXPERT SKILLS

BOOK 4: NMAP BEYOND BOUNDARIES: MASTERING COMPLEX NETWORK RECONNAISSANCE

Introduction

Welcome to the "NMAP Network Scanning Series" and the "Network Security, Monitoring, and Scanning Library," a comprehensive collection of books designed to empower you with the knowledge and skills needed to navigate the intricate world of network security and reconnaissance. In an age where the digital realm has become an integral part of our daily lives, the importance of safeguarding our networks and data cannot be overstated. This book bundle serves as your guiding light on the journey towards network security excellence.

In a rapidly evolving cybersecurity landscape, staying ahead of potential threats and vulnerabilities is a constant challenge. With the "NMAP Network Scanning Series," we aim to equip both beginners and seasoned professionals with the essential tools and expertise required to protect, monitor, and secure their networks effectively.

This bundle comprises four distinct volumes, each building upon the foundation laid by its predecessor. Whether you are just starting your journey in the world of network scanning or seeking to master advanced techniques, this series offers a comprehensive roadmap to help you achieve your goals.

"Book 1: NMAP for Beginners" serves as an entry point, providing a practical and hands-on introduction to network scanning. With a focus on foundational concepts and easy-to-follow instructions, this book is perfect for those new to the field.
As we progress to "Book 2: NMAP Mastery," we delve deeper into advanced techniques and strategies for network analysis. Here, you will unlock the secrets of NMAP scripting, customized

scanning, and gain the skills needed to perform in-depth network assessments.

"Book 3: NMAP Security Essentials" underscores the importance of network protection. This volume guides you through expert-level skills, helping you secure your network infrastructure, analyze firewall rules, and harden network devices.

Finally, "Book 4: NMAP Beyond Boundaries" explores the frontiers of complex network reconnaissance. Geospatial mapping, IoT security, cloud scanning, and web application assessment are just a few of the advanced topics covered, making this book an invaluable resource for those seeking to tackle intricate network challenges.

Whether you are an IT professional, network administrator, cybersecurity enthusiast, or anyone concerned with the security and integrity of networked systems, the "NMAP Network Scanning Series" and the "Network Security, Monitoring, and Scanning Library" have been meticulously crafted to meet your needs. Each book is designed to be informative, practical, and transformative, empowering you with the skills required to protect and secure your networks.

We invite you to embark on this educational journey with us, as together, we explore the ever-evolving world of network security and monitoring. Let this bundle be your companion in mastering the art of network scanning, securing your digital assets, and navigating the complexities of the modern cybersecurity landscape.

BOOK 1
NMAP FOR BEGINNERS
A PRACTICAL GUIDE TO NETWORK SCANNING

ROB BOTWRIGHT

Chapter 1: Introduction to Network Scanning

Scanning fundamentals are essential in understanding the core principles of network reconnaissance. Network scanning, at its core, involves the systematic exploration of computer networks to identify open ports, active hosts, and services running on those hosts. The knowledge gained through scanning is vital for network administrators and security professionals to maintain network integrity and assess potential vulnerabilities.

Network scanning can be executed using various tools, but one of the most popular and versatile tools is NMAP, which stands for Network Mapper. NMAP is a command-line tool that provides a comprehensive set of options for network scanning and analysis. To initiate a basic NMAP scan, you simply open your terminal or command prompt and enter the "nmap" command followed by the target's IP address or hostname.

For example, to scan a host with the IP address 192.168.1.1, you would type:

nmap 192.168.1.1

This command will instruct NMAP to perform a default scan on the specified target. The default scan includes host discovery and a basic scan of the most common 1,000 ports on the target system. The results are then displayed on your screen, showing which ports are open and what services are running on those ports.

NMAP uses various scanning techniques to gather information about a network. One of the most common techniques is the "TCP connect" scan, which establishes a full TCP connection to each port being scanned. This method is reliable but also quite noisy, as it generates a significant amount of traffic that may be detected by intrusion detection systems (IDS) or intrusion prevention systems (IPS).

Another scanning technique is the "SYN scan" or "half-open scan," which sends a SYN packet to the target port and waits for a response. If the port is open, it responds with a SYN-ACK, and NMAP records it as an open port. If the port is closed, it responds with a RST-ACK, indicating that the port is closed. The SYN scan is faster and less detectable than a TCP connect scan.

In addition to these fundamental scanning techniques, NMAP offers advanced options to gather more detailed information about the target network. These options include service version detection, OS fingerprinting, and scriptable scanning with the NMAP Scripting Engine (NSE). By leveraging these capabilities, NMAP can provide valuable insights into the target network's configuration and potential vulnerabilities.

Understanding the results of a network scan is equally important as conducting the scan itself. NMAP provides clear and concise output that includes information about open ports, services, operating system details, and script results (if applicable). Network administrators and security professionals can analyze this information to assess the network's security posture and take appropriate actions to mitigate risks.

It's important to note that while network scanning is a valuable tool for security professionals and network administrators, it should always be conducted responsibly and ethically. Unauthorized scanning of networks that you do not own or have explicit permission to scan is illegal and unethical. Always ensure you have the necessary permissions before initiating any network scanning activities.

In summary, scanning fundamentals are the building blocks of network reconnaissance. NMAP, as a versatile and powerful tool, plays a crucial role in network scanning by providing a wide range of scanning techniques and options. Understanding how to use NMAP effectively and responsibly is essential for network administrators and security professionals to maintain network security and assess vulnerabilities accurately.

Network scanning is an integral component of modern cybersecurity strategies, serving as a fundamental practice in safeguarding digital assets and maintaining the integrity of computer networks. It is essential for organizations and individuals alike to comprehend the significance of network scanning, as it underpins a proactive approach to network security, vulnerability assessment, and risk management.

At its core, network scanning is the process of systematically examining a network's infrastructure to identify and evaluate potential vulnerabilities, weaknesses, and security risks. This proactive approach empowers network administrators and security professionals to detect and address vulnerabilities before malicious actors exploit them for unauthorized access or data breaches.

The importance of network scanning lies in its ability to provide a comprehensive view of a network's topology, device configuration, and open ports. By conducting regular scans, organizations can gain insights into their network's current state, which is crucial for making informed decisions regarding security measures and updates.

Network scanning can be initiated using various tools and techniques, with NMAP being a widely recognized and versatile tool for the job. To execute a basic NMAP scan, one typically opens a command-line interface (CLI) and enters the "nmap" command followed by the target's IP address or hostname.

For example, to scan a host with the IP address 192.168.1.1, one would enter:

nmap 192.168.1.1

This simple CLI command instructs NMAP to conduct a default scan on the specified target. The default scan includes host discovery and a scan of the most common 1,000 ports on the target system. The results are then presented in a comprehensible format, allowing administrators to assess the network's security posture.

Network scanning is not a one-time event but an ongoing process. Regular scans are essential because networks are dynamic, with changes occurring due to software updates, device additions, or configuration modifications. Regular scans help ensure that vulnerabilities are promptly identified and addressed.

One of the key benefits of network scanning is its role in vulnerability assessment. By scanning a network, organizations can pinpoint weak points that might be exploited by cybercriminals. Vulnerability assessment is a crucial aspect of risk management, as it enables organizations to prioritize security efforts and allocate resources effectively to mitigate potential threats.

NMAP, as a powerful network scanning tool, offers several scanning techniques and options to gather detailed information about the target network. These advanced options include service version detection, OS fingerprinting, and scriptable scanning through the NMAP Scripting Engine (NSE). Leveraging these capabilities, NMAP can provide valuable insights into a network's configuration and potential vulnerabilities.

Furthermore, network scanning is essential for compliance with security regulations and standards. Many industries, such as finance and healthcare, are subject to stringent regulatory requirements regarding network security. Regular scans and vulnerability assessments are often mandated to demonstrate compliance with these regulations and to avoid potential fines or legal consequences.

While network scanning is a valuable tool for security professionals and network administrators, it must be conducted responsibly and ethically. Unauthorized scanning of networks that one does not own or have explicit permission to scan is both illegal and unethical. It is imperative to adhere to legal and ethical guidelines and obtain the necessary permissions before initiating any network scanning activities.

In summary, the importance of network scanning cannot be overstated in the realm of modern cybersecurity. It serves as a proactive approach to network security, vulnerability assessment, and risk management. By regularly conducting network scans and leveraging powerful tools like NMAP, organizations can maintain the integrity of their networks, detect vulnerabilities, and stay compliant with industry regulations. Responsible and ethical network scanning practices are essential for protecting digital assets and sensitive information in an increasingly interconnected world.

Chapter 2: Setting Up Your NMAP Environment

The installation of NMAP, or Network Mapper, is the first step towards harnessing the powerful capabilities of this open-source network scanning tool. To install NMAP, you'll need to navigate to the official NMAP website or use your system's package manager, depending on your operating system.

For Linux users, you can often install NMAP via the package manager specific to your distribution. For example, on Debian-based systems like Ubuntu, you can use the following CLI command:

arduino

sudo apt-get install nmap

On Red Hat-based systems like CentOS, you can use the "yum" package manager:

sudo yum install nmap

Alternatively, for Linux, you can compile NMAP from source code, which allows you to customize the installation to suit your specific requirements. To do this, you'll need to download the NMAP source code from the official website and follow the provided instructions for building and installing it.

For Windows users, NMAP provides a Windows installer executable (an .exe file) on their website. Simply download the installer and follow the on-screen instructions to install NMAP on your Windows machine.

Mac users can use package managers like Homebrew or MacPorts to install NMAP. If you prefer Homebrew, you can use the following CLI command:

brew install nmap

Once NMAP is installed on your system, you can verify its installation by running the following command:

nmap --version

This command will display the installed NMAP version and confirm that the installation was successful.

Installing NMAP is a straightforward process, but it opens the door to a world of network scanning and reconnaissance capabilities. Whether you're a network administrator, security professional, or simply interested in exploring your network's structure and vulnerabilities, NMAP is a valuable tool that can provide you with valuable insights and help you maintain network security.

Configuring NMAP for your specific environment is a crucial step to ensure that this powerful network scanning tool performs effectively and efficiently. The default configuration of NMAP may not always suit your needs, as network environments vary widely in terms of complexity and requirements.

To configure NMAP for your environment, you should first understand the specific goals of your network scanning tasks. Are you performing a basic network discovery to identify active hosts? Are you conducting a detailed vulnerability assessment? Are you scanning a local network or a remote network segment?

Once you've defined your scanning objectives, you can start customizing NMAP's settings accordingly. One important aspect of NMAP configuration is specifying the target or range of IP addresses you want to scan.

You can do this by providing the target IP address(es) as an argument when running NMAP from the command line. For example, to scan a single host with the IP address 192.168.1.1, you would use the following CLI command:

nmap 192.168.1.1

If you want to scan a range of IP addresses, you can use CIDR notation. For instance, to scan all hosts in the 192.168.1.0/24 subnet, you would use the following command:

nmap 192.168.1.0/24

Additionally, you can specify multiple targets separated by spaces, like this:

nmap 192.168.1.1 192.168.1.2

Once you have defined your target(s), you can customize the scanning techniques and options based on your specific requirements. NMAP offers various scan types, including the default scan, which is a comprehensive scan of the most common 1,000 ports, and more advanced scans, such as the SYN scan, which is faster and stealthier.

The choice of scan type depends on factors like the network size, the presence of intrusion detection systems (IDS) or intrusion prevention systems (IPS), and the level of detail you need in the scan results. For example, if you want a quick overview of active hosts and open ports, a SYN scan may be suitable:

nmap -sS 192.168.1.0/24

To perform a more comprehensive scan with service version detection, you can use the following command:

nmap -sV 192.168.1.0/24

Another crucial aspect of NMAP configuration is specifying the scan timing and performance options. NMAP allows you to control the speed of the scan to avoid overwhelming the target network or triggering network security alerts.

You can adjust the timing with options like "-T0" for Paranoid, "-T1" for Sneaky, "-T2" for Polite, "-T3" for Normal (default), "-T4" for Aggressive, and "-T5" for Insane. For example, to use the Aggressive timing template, you would enter the following command:

nmap -T4 192.168.1.0/24

Furthermore, NMAP provides the ability to save scan results in various formats, such as XML, grepable, and normal (human-readable) output. You can specify the desired output format with the "-o" option. For instance, to save scan results in XML format, you would use the following command:

nmap -oX scan_results.xml 192.168.1.0/24

Additionally, NMAP allows you to customize scans further by using scripting and NMAP Scripting Engine (NSE). You can write custom NSE scripts or leverage existing scripts to automate specific tasks, conduct more advanced scans, or perform additional network reconnaissance.

To use a specific NSE script, you can specify it with the "--script" option, like this:

nmap --script vuln 192.168.1.0/24

In this example, NMAP would run the "vuln" script against the specified targets to identify vulnerabilities.

Customizing NMAP for your environment is essential for efficient and effective network scanning. By understanding your network's requirements, specifying target IP addresses, choosing the appropriate scan types, adjusting scan timing, and utilizing scripting capabilities, you can tailor NMAP to meet your specific goals and gather valuable insights about your network's security posture.

Chapter 3: Understanding NMAP Syntax

Understanding the NMAP command structure is fundamental to harnessing the full power of this versatile network scanning tool. NMAP's command-line interface (CLI) provides a flexible and comprehensive set of options that allow you to customize your network scans to meet specific objectives.

At its core, an NMAP command consists of the "nmap" command followed by various options and arguments. The basic syntax of an NMAP command is as follows:

nmap [Scan Type] [Options] [Target]

The "Scan Type" refers to the specific type of scan you want to perform, such as a SYN scan, UDP scan, or comprehensive scan. For instance, if you want to conduct a SYN scan, you would specify it as the scan type with the "-sS" option:

nmap -sS [Options] [Target]

The "Options" section allows you to fine-tune your scan by specifying various parameters. NMAP offers a wide range of options to control scan timing, output format, verbosity, and more. For example, you can use the "-T4" option to set the timing template to Aggressive for faster scans:

nmap -sS -T4 [Target]

Additionally, you can use the "-oA" option to save scan results in all formats (XML, grepable, and normal) in one command:

nmap -sS -oA scan_results [Target]

The "Target" section of the command specifies the target or range of IP addresses you want to scan. You can specify a single IP address, a hostname, a range of IP addresses using CIDR notation, or even a list of targets separated by spaces.

For example, to scan a single host with the IP address 192.168.1.1, you would enter:

nmap -sS 192.168.1.1

To scan a range of IP addresses, such as the 192.168.1.0/24 subnet, you can use:

nmap -sS 192.168.1.0/24

NMAP provides a variety of scan types, each tailored to specific needs. For instance, the SYN scan (-sS) is a stealthy and fast scan that sends SYN packets to target ports and listens for responses, making it suitable for initial network reconnaissance.

The UDP scan (-sU) is used to identify open UDP ports, which are commonly associated with services like DNS, DHCP, and SNMP. By sending UDP packets to various ports, NMAP determines which ones are open and responsive.

For more comprehensive scans, the "-sC" option allows you to run NMAP scripts, and the "-sV" option enables service version detection, helping you identify the software and its version running on open ports.

Another important aspect of the NMAP command structure is the use of timing templates. Timing templates, specified with the "-T" option, control the speed of the scan and help avoid overwhelming the target network or triggering security alerts.

NMAP provides several timing templates, including "Paranoid," "Sneaky," "Polite," "Normal," "Aggressive," and "Insane." The choice of timing template depends on factors like network size, network environment, and the level of detail needed in the scan results.

For example, you can use the Aggressive timing template (-T4) for faster scans in a well-monitored network:

nmap -sS -T4 [Target]

However, if you want to maintain a low profile and avoid detection, the Paranoid timing template (-T0) is a suitable choice:

nmap -sS -T0 [Target]

Another important option is the choice of output format. NMAP allows you to save scan results in various formats, such as XML, grepable, and normal output (human-readable).

You can specify the desired output format using options like "-oX" for XML, "-oG" for grepable, and "-oN" for normal output.

For example, to save scan results in XML format, you would use the following command:

nmap -sS -oX scan_results .xml [Target]

By understanding the NMAP command structure and its various options, you can tailor your network scans to suit specific objectives, whether it's basic host discovery, in-depth vulnerability assessment, or service version detection. This flexibility and versatility make NMAP a valuable tool for network administrators, security professionals, and anyone seeking to gain insights into their network's configuration and potential security risks.

When using NMAP, it's essential to understand and leverage the common options available to customize your network scans effectively. These options allow you to fine-tune your scans, specify scan types, control timing, and format the output to meet your specific needs.

One of the most fundamental options is the "-p" option, which allows you to specify the port range you want to scan. For example, if you want to scan ports 80, 443, and 8080 on a target with the IP address 192.168.1.1, you can use the following command:

`nmap -p 80,443,8080 192.168.1.1`

Alternatively, you can specify a port range using a hyphen, like this:

`nmap -p 80-100 192.168.1.1`

The "-F" option is another useful option that performs a fast scan by scanning only the most common 100 ports. This option is suitable for quickly identifying open ports on a target:

r

`nmap -F 192.168.1.1`

NMAP offers options to control the verbosity of the scan output, allowing you to adjust the level of detail in the results. The "-v" option increases the verbosity level, providing more information about the scan progress and results:

`nmap -v 192.168.1.1`

Conversely, the "-q" option enables quiet mode, reducing the amount of output displayed during the scan:

`nmap -q 192.168.1.1`

The "-A" option, often referred to as aggressive scanning, combines various scan types and scripts to provide comprehensive information about the target. It includes OS detection, service version detection, script scanning, and traceroute information:

nmap -A 192.168.1.1

NMAP also offers options to control scan timing and performance. The "-T" option allows you to specify the timing template, affecting the speed and aggressiveness of the scan. Options range from "-T0" (Paranoid) to "-T5" (Insane), with each template offering different levels of aggressiveness:

nmap -T3 192.168.1.1

For a more in-depth scan with service version detection and script scanning, you can use the "-T4" option for a balanced approach:

nmap -T4 192.168.1.1

To save scan results for further analysis or reporting, you can use the "-o" option to specify the output format. For example, to save scan results in XML format, you would use:

nmap -oX scan_results.xml 192.168.1.1

The "-oG" option generates grepable output, which can be useful for parsing scan results using other tools or scripts:

nmap -oG scan_results.grepable 192.168.1.1

NMAP also provides the option to scan a target multiple times at different intervals with the "-iR" option. This can be useful for randomized scanning to avoid detection and to gather a more comprehensive view of the target's availability and open ports:

nmap -iR 10

Another essential option is the "--script" option, which allows you to specify NMAP scripts for additional functionality during the scan. For example, to run a script that detects common vulnerabilities, you can use:

nmap --script vuln 192.168.1.1

NMAP's common options give you the flexibility and control needed to tailor your network scans to your specific objectives. Whether you're conducting a quick port scan, an aggressive comprehensive scan, or utilizing scripts for advanced functionality, understanding these options is key to effectively using NMAP for network reconnaissance and security assessment.

Chapter 4: Basic Network Discovery with NMAP

Host discovery, a fundamental aspect of network scanning, is the process of identifying active hosts within a network or a specific IP address range. It serves as the initial step in network reconnaissance, enabling network administrators and security professionals to determine which hosts are online and reachable.

NMAP, as a versatile network scanning tool, offers various host discovery techniques to achieve this objective. One of the most common host discovery methods is the ICMP Echo Request, also known as a ping request.

To initiate a host discovery scan using ICMP Echo Requests, you can use the following NMAP command:

nmap -sn 192.168.1.0/24

This command instructs NMAP to send ICMP Echo Requests to all IP addresses within the specified range (192.168.1.0/24) and report back the hosts that respond.

However, some hosts may be configured to block or ignore ICMP Echo Requests, rendering this method ineffective in certain situations. In such cases, NMAP provides alternative host discovery techniques.

Another host discovery technique is the ARP scan, which is especially useful in local networks. This scan leverages Address Resolution Protocol (ARP) requests to identify hosts within the same subnet.

To perform an ARP scan, you can use the following NMAP command:

nmap -PR 192.168.1.0/24

In this command, NMAP sends ARP requests to all IP addresses within the specified range (192.168.1.0/24) to determine the active hosts.

In addition to ICMP and ARP, NMAP offers other host discovery methods, such as TCP and UDP scans. These scans involve probing specific ports on target hosts to check for responsiveness.

A common TCP-based host discovery technique is the "ACK scan," which sends TCP ACK (Acknowledgment) packets to potential hosts. If a host responds with a RST (Reset) packet, it is considered active.

To perform an ACK scan for host discovery, you can use the following NMAP command:

nmap -PA 192.168.1.0/24

Similarly, UDP-based host discovery involves sending UDP packets to potential hosts and analyzing their responses. The "UDP scan" can help identify hosts that respond to UDP packets, indicating their presence.

To initiate a UDP scan for host discovery, you can use the following NMAP command:

nmap -PU 192.168.1.0/24

When conducting host discovery, it's essential to consider the network environment and the specific objectives of the scan. Certain host discovery techniques may be more suitable than others depending on factors like network size, firewall configurations, and the level of stealth required.

For example, ICMP and ARP scans are effective in local networks but may not be suitable for external network scanning due to potential firewall restrictions. In contrast, TCP and UDP scans can be useful in external network scanning, where ICMP traffic may be blocked.

Additionally, host discovery techniques like ARP scans are typically faster and more accurate within the local network, as they rely on broadcast messages to identify hosts. However, they may not be applicable in larger or segmented networks.

Furthermore, some host discovery methods, such as TCP and UDP scans, may generate more network traffic and potentially trigger intrusion detection systems (IDS) or intrusion prevention systems (IPS). It's crucial to consider the impact of these scans on the target network's stability and security.

In summary, host discovery is a critical step in network reconnaissance, allowing you to identify active hosts within a network or IP address range. NMAP provides various host discovery techniques, including ICMP, ARP, TCP, and UDP scans, to accommodate different network environments and scanning objectives. Choosing the right host discovery method depends on factors like network size, firewall configurations, and the level of stealth required for the scan.

Network mapping is a critical aspect of network reconnaissance that goes beyond identifying active hosts and open ports. It involves creating a comprehensive visual representation of a network's structure, topology, and connections, providing valuable insights into its configuration and potential vulnerabilities.

NMAP, a versatile network scanning tool, offers features and techniques to aid in network mapping. One of the fundamental tools used for network mapping is the "Topology Discovery" feature, which allows NMAP to identify and map network devices and their interconnections.

To perform a basic network mapping scan, you can use the following NMAP command:

nmap -sn -oA network_map 192.168.1.0/24

In this command, NMAP conducts a "ping scan" (-sn) to identify active hosts in the specified IP address range (192.168.1.0/24) and saves the results in various formats, including XML, grepable, and normal output.

The output files generated by this command can be further analyzed and visualized to create network maps. Visualization tools like NMAP's own Zenmap, Gephi, or specialized network mapping software can help transform the scan results into easily understandable network diagrams.

Network mapping provides several benefits, such as helping network administrators understand the network's structure and relationships between devices. It aids in identifying potential points of failure, optimizing network performance, and enhancing security by detecting unauthorized or rogue devices.

Another key aspect of network mapping is identifying network segments and subnets, which helps in managing IP address allocations and optimizing routing. By mapping out subnets and their corresponding devices, administrators can ensure efficient IP address allocation and routing configurations.

Furthermore, network mapping can uncover hidden or misconfigured devices that may pose security risks. For example, a device with default or weak credentials may go unnoticed in a network scan but could potentially be exploited by attackers. Network mapping can help detect such devices and prompt administrators to take action.

Additionally, network mapping assists in maintaining an up-to-date inventory of network assets, which is crucial for asset management and compliance purposes. By regularly mapping the network and comparing the results, organizations can track changes, additions, or removals of devices, ensuring that the network inventory remains accurate.

To perform more advanced network mapping, NMAP offers options to identify services running on open ports, providing additional details about network devices. The "-sV" option enables service version detection, helping administrators determine the specific software and versions in use.

For example, you can use the following NMAP command to perform a comprehensive scan that includes service version detection:

```
nmap -sS -sV -oA detailed_map 192.168.1.0/24
```

In this command, NMAP conducts a SYN scan (-sS) to identify open ports and services, along with service version detection (-sV) to gather detailed information about the services running on the target hosts.

The results of such scans can be used to create detailed network maps that include information about the types of services, software versions, and potential vulnerabilities.

When creating network maps, it's crucial to consider the security and privacy implications. Sensitive information, such as IP addresses, device names, and service details, should be protected and shared only with authorized personnel.

Network mapping can also uncover potential security weaknesses or misconfigurations, such as devices with default credentials, open ports, or unnecessary services. Administrators should use this information to secure the network and address any vulnerabilities promptly.

In summary, network mapping is a crucial practice in network reconnaissance, providing a comprehensive view of a network's structure, topology, and connections. NMAP offers valuable features and techniques for network mapping, enabling administrators to identify active hosts, subnets, and services, and create visual representations of the network. Effective network mapping helps optimize network performance, enhance security, and maintain an accurate inventory of network assets.

Chapter 5: Port Scanning and Service Detection

Port scanning techniques are a fundamental aspect of network reconnaissance, enabling the identification of open ports and services on target hosts. These techniques are essential for network administrators and security professionals seeking to assess the security and accessibility of devices within a network.

NMAP, a versatile network scanning tool, provides a range of port scanning options and techniques that cater to different scanning objectives and network environments. One of the most basic and commonly used port scanning techniques is the "TCP Connect Scan."

To perform a TCP Connect Scan with NMAP, you can use the following command:

nmap -sT [Target]

In this command, the "-sT" option instructs NMAP to conduct a TCP Connect Scan, which involves initiating a full three-way handshake with the target port to determine its state.

TCP Connect Scans are reliable and accurate but may be easily detected by intrusion detection systems (IDS) or intrusion prevention systems (IPS) due to their noisy nature. They involve opening a connection to each port, which can generate a considerable amount of network traffic.

To perform a more stealthy scan, the "TCP SYN Scan" is a preferred technique. It involves sending SYN (Synchronize) packets to the target ports without completing the handshake.

To initiate a TCP SYN Scan with NMAP, you can use the following command:

nmap -sS [Target]

The "-sS" option tells NMAP to perform a TCP SYN Scan, which is faster and generates less network traffic than a TCP Connect Scan.

TCP SYN Scans are often used in network reconnaissance because they are less likely to trigger security alerts. However, they may not provide as much information about the target's services and versions as a full handshake would.

Another port scanning technique is the "TCP FIN Scan," which involves sending TCP FIN (Finish) packets to the target ports. If a port is open, it should respond with an RST (Reset) packet.

To perform a TCP FIN Scan with NMAP, you can use the following command:

nmap -sF [Target]

The "-sF" option instructs NMAP to perform a TCP FIN Scan.

TCP FIN Scans can be useful for evading firewalls and intrusion detection systems. However, they may not work against all types of targets and may provide limited information compared to other scan types.

For identifying open UDP ports and services, the "UDP Scan" is a valuable technique. UDP scans involve sending UDP packets to the target ports and analyzing the responses.

To initiate a UDP Scan with NMAP, you can use the following command:

nmap -sU [Target]

The "-sU" option tells NMAP to perform a UDP Scan, which is useful for discovering services such as DNS, DHCP, and SNMP, which typically use UDP.

UDP Scans can be slower and less reliable than TCP scans, as UDP does not provide the same level of error checking and reliability as TCP. Additionally, some UDP services may not respond to scanning requests, making them challenging to identify.

A more advanced port scanning technique is the "XMAS Scan," which involves sending TCP packets with the FIN, URG, and PSH flags set. This technique relies on the behavior of various operating systems and their responses to such packets.

To perform an XMAS Scan with NMAP, you can use the following command:

nmap -sX [Target]

The "-sX" option instructs NMAP to perform an XMAS Scan.

XMAS Scans can be useful for identifying poorly configured or vulnerable systems. However, they may not work against all targets, and the results may be inconclusive in some cases.

To evade IDS and IPS systems further, the "TCP NULL Scan" sends TCP packets with no flags set, relying on how the target system responds to such packets.

To initiate a TCP NULL Scan with NMAP, you can use the following command:

nmap -sN [Target]

The "-sN" option tells NMAP to perform a TCP NULL Scan.

TCP NULL Scans can be stealthy, but their effectiveness depends on the target's behavior. Some systems may respond to NULL packets, while others may ignore them.

It's worth noting that while these port scanning techniques are valuable for network reconnaissance and vulnerability assessment, ethical considerations and compliance with applicable laws and regulations are essential. Unauthorized scanning of networks or systems without proper authorization is both unethical and illegal.

In summary, port scanning techniques are a critical part of network reconnaissance, enabling the identification of open ports and services on target hosts. NMAP provides a range of scanning options, including TCP Connect Scans, TCP SYN Scans, TCP FIN Scans, UDP Scans, XMAS Scans, TCP NULL Scans, and more, each with its advantages and considerations. Security professionals and network administrators must use these techniques responsibly and within legal and ethical boundaries.

Service detection methods are a critical aspect of network reconnaissance, providing insights into the types of services running on open ports. Understanding the services and their versions is essential for network administrators and security professionals to assess vulnerabilities and ensure network security.

NMAP, a versatile network scanning tool, offers several service detection methods to achieve this objective. One of the most common and straightforward methods is the "TCP Connect Scan" with service version detection.

To perform a TCP Connect Scan with service version detection using NMAP, you can use the following command:

nmap -sT -sV [Target]

In this command, the "-sT" option instructs NMAP to perform a TCP Connect Scan, while the "-sV" option enables service version detection.

TCP Connect Scans with service version detection involve initiating a full three-way handshake with open ports to determine the service type and version. This method is reliable but may be easily detected by intrusion detection systems (IDS) or intrusion prevention systems (IPS) due to its noisy nature.

For a more stealthy approach, the "TCP SYN Scan" with service version detection is a preferred technique. It involves sending SYN (Synchronize) packets to the target ports without completing the handshake.

To initiate a TCP SYN Scan with service version detection using NMAP, you can use the following command:

nmap -sS -sV [Target]

The "-sS" option tells NMAP to perform a TCP SYN Scan, while the "-sV" option enables service version detection.

TCP SYN Scans with service version detection are faster and generate less network traffic than TCP Connect Scans. They are less likely to trigger security alerts but may provide less detailed service information.

Another service detection method is the "UDP Scan" with service version detection. UDP scans involve sending UDP packets to target ports and analyzing their responses.

To initiate a UDP Scan with service version detection using NMAP, you can use the following command:

nmap -sU -sV [Target]

The "-sU" option instructs NMAP to perform a UDP Scan, while the "-sV" option enables service version detection.

UDP Scans with service version detection are valuable for discovering services such as DNS, DHCP, and SNMP, which typically use UDP. However, UDP scans can be slower and less reliable than TCP scans due to UDP's lack of error checking and reliability.

NMAP also provides the "Aggressive Service Detection" option, which combines multiple service detection techniques to gather comprehensive information about services and their versions.

To perform an Aggressive Service Detection scan using NMAP, you can use the following command:

nmap -A [Target]

The "-A" option enables Aggressive Service Detection, which includes OS detection, script scanning, and traceroute information in addition to service version detection.

Aggressive Service Detection scans provide a wealth of information about the target, making them valuable for in-depth network reconnaissance. However, they may be more likely to trigger security alerts and should be used with caution.

NMAP's service detection methods not only identify services but also determine their versions. Service version detection relies on NMAP's extensive database of service fingerprints, which contain patterns and characteristics unique to specific services and their versions.

When NMAP detects an open port, it sends service-specific probes to the target port and compares the responses to its database. Based on the responses, NMAP identifies the service and its version.

Service detection methods are valuable for network administrators and security professionals in various scenarios. They help identify the software running on target hosts, enabling administrators to apply appropriate patches and updates to secure the network.

Additionally, service detection assists in creating an accurate inventory of network assets by providing details about the services and their versions. This information is essential for asset management and compliance purposes.

Moreover, service detection methods are crucial for vulnerability assessment and penetration testing. By identifying services and their versions, security professionals can assess potential vulnerabilities and weaknesses, allowing for proactive security measures.

In summary, service detection methods are essential for network reconnaissance, providing insights into the types of services running on open ports. NMAP offers several service detection techniques, including TCP Connect Scans, TCP SYN Scans, UDP Scans, and Aggressive Service Detection, each with its advantages and considerations. These methods are valuable for network security, asset management, and vulnerability assessment, helping administrators and security professionals maintain a secure and well-managed network.

Chapter 6: Host Discovery Techniques

ICMP (Internet Control Message Protocol) is a fundamental network protocol that plays a crucial role in network communication. It is primarily used for diagnostic and control purposes, allowing devices to communicate error messages and other network-related information.

ICMP-based discovery, also known as ICMP scanning or ping scanning, is a host discovery technique that relies on ICMP Echo Requests and Echo Replies. This technique is a fundamental part of network reconnaissance, enabling the identification of active hosts within a network or IP address range.

To initiate an ICMP-based discovery scan using the NMAP tool, you can use the following command:

nmap -sn [Target]

In this command, the "-sn" option instructs NMAP to perform a "ping scan," which sends ICMP Echo Requests to the target IP addresses and records the responses.

ICMP-based discovery scans are efficient for quickly identifying active hosts, as most devices respond to ICMP Echo Requests. This technique is especially useful in local network environments and can provide a basic understanding of the network's structure.

However, it's essential to note that ICMP-based discovery has limitations. Some hosts and networks may block or restrict ICMP traffic for security reasons. In such cases, this technique may not be effective in identifying all active hosts.

ICMP-based discovery scans are relatively straightforward and lightweight in terms of network traffic. They do not involve probing specific ports or services, making them less likely to trigger intrusion detection systems (IDS) or intrusion prevention systems (IPS).

An advantage of ICMP-based discovery is its speed and efficiency, making it suitable for initial network reconnaissance to identify online hosts quickly. It is often used as a preliminary step in more extensive network scans, helping network administrators narrow down the list of hosts for further analysis.

ICMP-based discovery scans can be further customized to target specific IP address ranges or hosts. For example, you can perform an ICMP discovery scan on a specific subnet by specifying the subnet's IP range:

nmap -sn 192.168.1.0/24

In this command, NMAP scans all IP addresses within the 192.168.1.0/24 subnet, sending ICMP Echo Requests to each address and recording the responses.

Additionally, you can specify multiple target hosts or IP addresses in a single command, separated by spaces:

nmap -sn 192.168.1.1 192.168.1.2 192.168.1.3

ICMP-based discovery scans are an essential tool for network administrators and security professionals. They provide a quick and efficient way to identify active hosts within a network or IP address range, helping administrators understand the network's structure and availability.

While ICMP-based discovery scans are useful for initial reconnaissance, it's important to remember that they only provide information about host availability. They do not provide details about open ports, services, or vulnerabilities on the target hosts.

To gain a more comprehensive understanding of a network's security posture and potential vulnerabilities, administrators often complement ICMP-based discovery with other scanning techniques, such as port scanning and service detection.

In summary, ICMP-based discovery is a fundamental technique in network reconnaissance, allowing administrators to identify active hosts quickly. NMAP's "ping scan" option provides a simple and efficient way to perform ICMP-based discovery scans, making it a valuable tool for initial network reconnaissance and understanding network availability.

TCP (Transmission Control Protocol) is a core protocol of the Internet Protocol (IP) suite and is widely used for reliable data communication between devices on a network. In the context of network reconnaissance and host discovery, TCP-based techniques play a crucial role in identifying active hosts, open ports, and available services.

TCP-based host discovery techniques involve sending TCP packets to potential target hosts and analyzing their responses. These techniques help network administrators and security professionals determine which hosts are online and which ports are open, enabling them to assess network security and availability.

NMAP, a versatile network scanning tool, provides several TCP-based discovery methods, each with its advantages and considerations. One of the most common techniques is the "TCP Connect Scan."

To perform a TCP Connect Scan using NMAP, you can use the following command:

nmap -sT [Target]

In this command, the "-sT" option instructs NMAP to conduct a TCP Connect Scan, which involves initiating a full three-way handshake with the target ports to determine their state.

TCP Connect Scans are reliable and accurate, providing detailed information about open ports and services. However, they may be easily detected by intrusion detection systems (IDS) or intrusion prevention systems (IPS) due to their noisy nature, as they involve opening a connection to each port.

For a more stealthy approach, the "TCP SYN Scan" is a preferred TCP-based host discovery technique. It involves sending SYN (Synchronize) packets to the target ports without completing the handshake.

To initiate a TCP SYN Scan using NMAP, you can use the following command:

```
nmap -sS [Target]
```

The "-sS" option tells NMAP to perform a TCP SYN Scan, which is faster and generates less network traffic than a TCP Connect Scan. Additionally, SYN Scans are less likely to trigger security alerts.

TCP SYN Scans are especially useful in network reconnaissance, as they quickly identify open ports and potential services running on target hosts. However, they may not provide as much information about the target's services and versions as a full handshake would.

Another TCP-based host discovery technique is the "TCP FIN Scan," which involves sending TCP FIN (Finish) packets to the target ports. If a port is open, it should respond with an RST (Reset) packet.

To perform a TCP FIN Scan using NMAP, you can use the following command:

```
nmap -sF [Target]
```

The "-sF" option instructs NMAP to perform a TCP FIN Scan. TCP FIN Scans can be useful for evading firewalls and intrusion detection systems. However, they may not work against all types of targets, and the results may be inconclusive in some cases.

In addition to these techniques, NMAP offers a "TCP NULL Scan," which sends TCP packets with no flags set, relying on how the target system responds to such packets.

To initiate a TCP NULL Scan using NMAP, you can use the following command:

nmap -sN [Target]

The "-sN" option tells NMAP to perform a TCP NULL Scan.

TCP NULL Scans can be stealthy, but their effectiveness depends on the target's behavior. Some systems may respond to NULL packets, while others may ignore them.

Moreover, NMAP provides an "XMAS Scan" technique that involves sending TCP packets with the FIN, URG, and PSH flags set. This technique relies on the behavior of various operating systems and their responses to such packets.

To perform an XMAS Scan using NMAP, you can use the following command:

nmap -sX [Target]

The "-sX" option instructs NMAP to perform an XMAS Scan.

XMAS Scans can be valuable for identifying poorly configured or vulnerable systems. However, they may not work against all targets, and the results may be inconclusive in some cases.

It's essential to use TCP-based host discovery techniques responsibly and within legal and ethical boundaries. Unauthorized scanning of networks or systems without proper authorization is unethical and illegal.

In summary, TCP-based discovery techniques are essential for network reconnaissance, allowing network administrators and security professionals to identify active hosts and open ports. NMAP offers various TCP-based scanning methods, including TCP Connect Scans, TCP SYN Scans, TCP FIN Scans, TCP NULL Scans, and XMAS Scans, each with its strengths and considerations. Understanding these techniques is crucial for effective network reconnaissance and security assessment.

Chapter 7: NMAP Scripting Engine (NSE)

The NMAP Scripting Engine, often referred to as NSE, is a powerful and versatile feature of the NMAP network scanning tool. It extends NMAP's functionality by allowing users to write and execute custom scripts for a wide range of network reconnaissance and security tasks.

NSE scripts are written in the Lua programming language, a lightweight and efficient scripting language that is well-suited for network-related tasks. These scripts can be used to automate common network scanning and analysis tasks, making NMAP an even more valuable tool for network administrators and security professionals.

To utilize NSE scripts in NMAP, you can use the "--script" or "-sC" option followed by the name of the script or a category of scripts. For example, to run a specific script named "http-title," you can use the following command:

nmap --script http-title [Target]

Alternatively, you can use a category of scripts, such as "default," to execute a predefined set of scripts:

nmap -sC [Target]

The power of NSE lies in its ability to perform a wide variety of network reconnaissance tasks. For example, you can use NSE scripts to detect vulnerabilities, gather information about network services, identify open ports, and even automate complex tasks like brute-force password cracking.

One of the essential aspects of NSE is its extensive library of pre-built scripts that cover a wide range of network-related tasks and services. These scripts are maintained by the

NMAP community and are regularly updated to address new security issues and support the latest technologies.

As a network administrator or security professional, you can leverage NSE scripts to streamline your workflow and efficiently gather valuable information about target systems and networks. For example, you can use NSE scripts to identify web application vulnerabilities, retrieve banners from network services, or even enumerate SNMP information from devices.

One of the notable features of NSE is its scripting categories, which help organize and group related scripts for specific purposes. These categories include "default," "discovery," "exploit," "intrusive," "safe," and more, allowing users to choose scripts that align with their scanning objectives.

The "default" category, for instance, contains a set of commonly used scripts that provide basic information about target systems. Running scripts from this category is a good starting point for network reconnaissance.

In contrast, the "intrusive" category contains scripts that may perform more aggressive actions, such as attempting to brute-force passwords or exploiting vulnerabilities. These scripts should be used with caution and proper authorization, as they can generate significant network traffic and potentially disrupt services.

To explore the available NSE scripts and categories, you can use the following command:

nmap --script-help

This command displays a list of script categories and descriptions, helping you identify scripts that suit your scanning objectives.

Customizing NSE scripts is another valuable aspect of NMAP's scripting capabilities. You can modify existing scripts or create entirely new ones tailored to your specific network reconnaissance and security needs.

Custom scripting allows you to automate tasks that are unique to your network environment or organization. For example, you can create scripts to check for compliance with internal security policies or perform specialized network audits.

Writing NSE scripts in Lua is accessible to both experienced programmers and those with limited scripting knowledge. The Lua language is known for its simplicity and readability, making it a suitable choice for writing custom scripts for NMAP.

While NSE scripts provide a vast array of functionality, it's crucial to use them responsibly and within legal and ethical boundaries. Unauthorized scanning or exploitation of systems and networks is both unethical and illegal.

Furthermore, it's essential to obtain proper authorization before using NSE scripts in a network environment. Network administrators should ensure that they have the necessary permissions to conduct scanning and testing activities.

In summary, the NMAP Scripting Engine (NSE) is a valuable feature of the NMAP network scanning tool that enhances its capabilities by allowing users to write and execute custom scripts for network reconnaissance and security tasks. NSE scripts are written in the Lua programming language and can automate a wide range of tasks, from identifying vulnerabilities to gathering information about network services. They are organized into categories, making it easy to choose scripts that align with specific scanning objectives. Custom scripting in NSE allows users to tailor scripts to their unique network environment and security requirements. However, responsible and ethical use of NSE scripts, along with proper authorization, is essential to ensure compliance with legal and ethical standards.

Writing custom NSE (NMAP Scripting Engine) scripts is a powerful way to extend the functionality of the NMAP network scanning tool to meet specific network reconnaissance and security requirements. Custom scripts allow network administrators and security professionals to automate tasks that may not be covered by pre-built scripts or to tailor existing scripts to their unique needs.

To create custom NSE scripts, you need to have a basic understanding of the Lua programming language, which is the scripting language used for NSE. Lua is known for its simplicity and readability, making it accessible to both experienced programmers and those with limited scripting knowledge.

Before diving into script writing, it's essential to have a clear understanding of the task or objective you want to achieve. Defining the scope and purpose of your custom script will guide your script development process.

The first step in writing a custom NSE script is to choose a suitable text editor or Integrated Development Environment (IDE) for writing Lua code. Popular choices include Notepad++, Visual Studio Code, or even a simple text editor like Vim or Nano.

Once you have your preferred text editor set up, you can start writing your custom NSE script. Begin by creating a new Lua file with a ".nse" extension, which indicates that it's an NSE script.

For example, if you want to create a custom NSE script to check for open FTP servers and retrieve banner information, you can start by creating a file named "ftp-banner.nse."

In the script file, you'll begin with a script description and author information to provide context for the script's purpose and its creator. This information is essential for documentation and attribution.

Here's an example of the script header with description and author information:

lua

-- Description: Custom NSE script to check for open FTP servers and retrieve banner information. -- Author: Your Name

Next, you'll define the script's categories, arguments, and dependencies. Categories help organize scripts, making it easier to locate and run them when needed. Arguments allow users to customize script behavior, and dependencies specify other scripts or libraries required for your script to function correctly.

Here's an example of script categories, arguments, and dependencies:

lua

categories = {"discovery", "safe"} arguments = { { name = "ftp-port", type = "number", default = 21, help = "FTP port to scan" }, { name = "output-file", type = "string", help = "File to save FTP banner information" } } dependencies = {"ftp-brute"}

In this example, the script is categorized under "discovery" and "safe," takes two arguments (FTP port and output file), and specifies a dependency on the "ftp-brute" script.

The next step is to define the script's main function, which contains the Lua code to perform the desired network reconnaissance task. For our FTP banner retrieval script, we'll create a function called "ftp_banner."

Here's an example of the script's main function:

lua

local function ftp_banner(host, port, output_file) local banner = nmap.get_banner(host, port) if banner then if output_file then local file = io.open(output_file, "a") if

file then file:write(host.ip, ":", port, "\t", banner, "\n")
file:close() else return false, "Failed to open output file"
end else return banner end end return true end

In this example, the "ftp_banner" function retrieves the FTP banner for the specified host and port. If an output file is provided, it appends the banner information to the file.

Finally, you'll register the script with NMAP by specifying the script's name, description, categories, arguments, and the main function to execute.

Here's an example of script registration:

lua

action = function(host, port, output_file) return ftp_banner(host, port, output_file) end

In this example, the "action" field specifies the main function to execute when the script is run.

Once you've written and saved your custom NSE script, you can use it with NMAP by specifying its name in the "--script" or "-sC" option, followed by any required arguments.

For example, to run the custom "ftp-banner.nse" script, you can use the following command:

nmap --script ftp-banner --script-args ftp-port=21,output-file=ftp_banners.txt [Target]

This command runs the custom script, specifying the FTP port to scan (default is 21) and the output file to save banner information.

Custom NSE scripts provide immense flexibility in tailoring NMAP's capabilities to specific network reconnaissance and security tasks. They can automate tasks, retrieve valuable information, and extend NMAP's functionality to meet unique requirements.

When writing custom NSE scripts, it's essential to follow best practices, including proper script documentation, error handling, and testing. Documentation helps others understand the script's purpose and usage, while error handling ensures robustness and reliability. Testing the script in various network environments helps ensure its effectiveness and accuracy.

In summary, writing custom NSE scripts is a valuable skill that allows network administrators and security professionals to extend NMAP's capabilities for specific network reconnaissance and security tasks. To create custom scripts, you'll need to have a basic understanding of Lua, choose a suitable text editor or IDE, define the script's scope and objectives, and follow best practices for script development. Once your custom script is written, you can register it with NMAP and use it alongside pre-built scripts to enhance your network reconnaissance and security assessments.

Chapter 8: NMAP Output and Reporting

Interpreting NMAP output is a crucial skill for network administrators and security professionals, as it provides valuable insights into the state of networked systems. NMAP, a powerful network scanning tool, generates detailed reports and information about the hosts, ports, services, and vulnerabilities discovered during a scan.

When you run an NMAP scan, the tool sends probes and collects responses from the target hosts and ports, generating a report that is typically presented in the command-line interface. Understanding and making sense of this report is essential for effective network reconnaissance and security assessments.

NMAP output is organized into sections, with each section containing specific information about the scan results. The first section usually includes a summary of the scan, showing the scan type, target hosts, and scan duration.

For example, after running an NMAP scan, you might see output like this:

kotlin

Nmap scan report for 192.168.1.1 Host is up (0.0010s latency). Not shown: 999 closed ports PORT STATE SERVICE 80/tcp open http

In this example, the first line provides information about the target host (192.168.1.1), indicating that it is up with low latency. Below that, you can see a summary of open ports and services, such as port 80 being open for HTTP.

The "PORT" column lists the open ports discovered during the scan, while the "STATE" column describes the state of each port (e.g., "open" for accessible ports).

NMAP also provides information about the services running on open ports, which can be found in the "SERVICE" column. This information is valuable for identifying the type and version of services on the target host.

NMAP offers different scanning techniques, and the output may vary depending on the scan type. For example, a basic TCP Connect Scan might produce a more straightforward report, while an in-depth service version detection scan provides detailed service information.

To interpret NMAP output effectively, it's essential to understand the different states that ports can be in. Common port states include "open" (the port is accessible and accepting connections), "closed" (the port is not actively listening for connections), and "filtered" (the port is blocked or not responding).

NMAP also provides additional information, such as the reason a port is in a specific state, the version of the service running on a port, and the service's name. These details can help administrators and security professionals assess the target system's security posture and potential vulnerabilities. In addition to open ports and services, NMAP output often includes information about the target host's operating system (OS) and its guess about the OS version. NMAP uses various techniques, such as OS fingerprinting and analysis of responses to specific probes, to make educated guesses about the target OS.

Here's an example of NMAP output that includes OS detection:

OS details: Linux 4.4 - 4.18, Linux 2.6.32 - 4.9, Linux 2.6.32 - 2.6.35

In this example, NMAP has identified the target host as likely running a Linux-based OS, with a range of possible kernel versions.

NMAP's output also provides information about script scanning results. Script scanning involves running NSE (NMAP Scripting Engine) scripts to gather additional information about the target system, such as potential vulnerabilities or configuration details.

Here's an example of NMAP output that includes script scanning results:

kotlin

Nmap scan report for 192.168.1.1 Host is up (0.0010s latency). Not shown: 999 closed ports PORT STATE SERVICE 80/tcp open http |_http-title: Example Website

In this example, NMAP has run an NSE script that retrieves the title of the HTTP service on port 80, revealing that it's an "Example Website."

Understanding NMAP's output requires not only familiarity with its formatting but also the ability to interpret the information in the context of your specific network reconnaissance or security assessment goals. You may need to correlate the discovered services with known vulnerabilities, prioritize further testing, or adjust your security measures based on the findings.

Moreover, NMAP provides options for generating output in various formats, including text, XML, and even interactive formats. Choosing the right format for your needs and using tools like grep or awk to parse and filter the output can make the interpretation process more efficient.

In summary, interpreting NMAP output is a vital skill for network administrators and security professionals, as it provides critical information about target hosts, open ports, services, and potential vulnerabilities. NMAP's output is organized into sections, including a summary, port states, service information, OS detection, and script scanning results. Understanding port states, service details, and OS information is essential for assessing a target system's security posture. Script scanning can further enhance the depth of information obtained during an NMAP scan. By effectively interpreting NMAP output, professionals can make informed decisions to secure their networks and systems effectively.

Creating NMAP reports is a critical step in documenting and communicating the results of your network reconnaissance and security assessments. NMAP, a powerful network scanning tool, generates detailed scan output, and transforming this output into structured reports can help you and your team understand the findings and take appropriate actions.

NMAP provides various options for generating reports in different formats, such as text, XML, and even interactive formats like Zenmap. The choice of report format depends on your specific needs and the audience for the report.

To create an NMAP report, you can use the "--o" or "--output" option, followed by the desired output filename. For example, to save the scan results in a text file named "scan_report.txt," you can use the following command:

nmap -oN scan_report.txt [Target]

In this command, the "-oN" option specifies the output format as a normal text file.

If you prefer XML output for more structured and machine-readable reports, you can use the "-oX" option:

nmap -oX scan_report.xml [Target]

This command generates an XML report named "scan_report.xml."

XML reports are often used when you need to process the scan results programmatically or integrate them with other tools or systems.

Another option for generating human-readable and interactive reports is to use the Zenmap graphical user interface, which is a front-end for NMAP. Zenmap allows you to run scans and create reports with a user-friendly interface.

To generate a report using Zenmap, follow these steps:

Launch Zenmap.

Enter the target IP address or hostname in the "Target" field.

Configure scan options and parameters as needed.

Click the "Scan" button to start the scan.

Once the scan is complete, click the "Scan" menu and select "Save Scan."

Choose the desired report format (e.g., Text, XML, or HTML) and specify the output filename and location.

Click the "Save" button to generate the report.

Zenmap provides a convenient way to run scans, customize options, and create reports without needing to use the command-line interface.

When creating NMAP reports, it's essential to consider the content and structure of the report. A well-structured report should include the following elements:

Scan Summary: Provide an overview of the scan, including the target hosts, scan type, and duration.

Host Information: List the discovered hosts and their details, such as IP addresses, hostnames, and open ports.

Port States: Present the states of scanned ports, including "open," "closed," or "filtered."

Service Information: Include information about services running on open ports, such as service names, versions, and banners.

Operating System Detection: If applicable, include the results of OS detection, which provides insights into the target's OS and version.

Script Scan Results: If NSE scripts were used during the scan, report the results, including script names and output.

Vulnerability Assessment: If vulnerabilities were identified during the scan, report them along with their severity and potential impact.

Recommendations: Provide recommendations and action items based on the scan findings, suggesting steps to improve network security.

Appendix: Include additional information, such as the command-line used for the scan, scan options, and any notes or observations.

Creating clear and concise reports is essential for effective communication with stakeholders, including colleagues, clients, or management. Reports should focus on relevant findings, avoid unnecessary technical details, and provide actionable insights.

It's also a good practice to include appropriate headings, formatting, and visual elements, such as tables or charts, to enhance readability and comprehension.

When documenting vulnerabilities or security issues in the report, it's essential to follow a standardized format. Include details such as the vulnerability name, CVE (Common Vulnerabilities and Exposures) identifier if available, severity level, and a brief description of the issue.

Moreover, consider categorizing vulnerabilities based on their impact and providing recommendations for remediation. This helps prioritize and address security concerns effectively.

While creating NMAP reports, keep in mind that they serve as a valuable reference for future assessments, audits, or security improvements. Well-documented reports enable you to track changes in the network environment over time, monitor the resolution of vulnerabilities, and assess the effectiveness of security measures.

Additionally, reports can be shared with other team members, security analysts, or auditors to ensure transparency and collaboration in addressing network security concerns.

In summary, creating NMAP reports is an essential step in network reconnaissance and security assessments. NMAP offers various output formats, including text, XML, and interactive reports through Zenmap. Structured reports should include a scan summary, host information, port states, service details, operating system detection, script scan results, vulnerability assessment, recommendations, and relevant appendix information. Clear and concise reports enhance communication and help stakeholders understand network security findings and take appropriate actions. Following standardized formats for vulnerabilities and maintaining a well-documented report history are essential practices in network security assessments.

Chapter 9: Network Vulnerability Assessment

Identifying vulnerable services is a critical aspect of network security assessments and penetration testing. In the ever-evolving landscape of cybersecurity threats, knowing which services on your network are susceptible to attacks is essential for proactive defense and remediation.

NMAP, a versatile network scanning tool, provides several techniques and methods to identify vulnerable services within your network. By scanning target hosts and analyzing their responses, NMAP can help you pinpoint services with known vulnerabilities that attackers could potentially exploit.

One of the fundamental techniques for identifying vulnerable services is through version detection. NMAP can query open ports to determine the specific versions of services running on them. This information is valuable because it allows you to cross-reference service versions with known vulnerabilities from databases like the National Vulnerability Database (NVD) or vendor-specific security advisories.

To perform version detection with NMAP, you can use the "-sV" option, followed by the target hosts:

nmap -sV [Target]

NMAP will send probes to open ports, collect responses, and attempt to identify the service and its version. The output will include information about the service version, which you can use to check for known vulnerabilities.

Another technique for identifying vulnerable services is by using NSE (NMAP Scripting Engine) scripts. NSE scripts are custom scripts that can automate various network reconnaissance tasks, including vulnerability assessment. NMAP provides a wide range of pre-built NSE scripts that can help identify vulnerabilities in specific services.

To run NSE scripts for vulnerability assessment, you can use the "--script" or "-sC" option, along with the target hosts:

nmap --script [Script] [Target]

Replace "[Script]" with the name of the NSE script you want to run. For example, to check for vulnerabilities in HTTP services, you can use the "http-vuln-cve2017-5638.nse" script:

nmap --script http-vuln-cve2017-5638 [Target]

NSE scripts like this one can help identify vulnerabilities in specific services by sending probes or known exploits and analyzing the responses. They often provide valuable information about the vulnerabilities, including their CVE (Common Vulnerabilities and Exposures) identifiers.

Additionally, you can use the "--script-args" option to customize the behavior of NSE scripts. For example, you can specify parameters to fine-tune the script's vulnerability checks.

When identifying vulnerable services with NMAP, it's essential to consider the context and potential impact of the vulnerabilities. Not all vulnerabilities are equally critical, and some may pose a more significant risk to your network than others. To prioritize remediation efforts, you can assess the severity and exploitability of the identified vulnerabilities.

One way to assess the severity of vulnerabilities is by checking their CVSS (Common Vulnerability Scoring System) scores. CVSS scores provide a standardized way to measure the impact and exploitability of vulnerabilities. Higher scores indicate more severe vulnerabilities, while lower scores suggest less critical issues.

To check the CVSS scores of identified vulnerabilities, you can use online databases or vulnerability assessment tools that provide this information. These databases often include detailed descriptions of vulnerabilities, their impact, and recommended remediation steps.

In addition to CVSS scores, you should consider the potential impact of vulnerabilities on your network. Some vulnerabilities may allow remote code execution, privilege escalation, or unauthorized access to sensitive data. Assessing the potential consequences of exploitation is essential for risk management.

After identifying vulnerable services and assessing their severity, you can take steps to remediate or mitigate the risks. Remediation may involve applying security patches, updates, or configuration changes to eliminate vulnerabilities. In cases where immediate patching is not possible, you can implement compensating controls or security measures to reduce the risk of exploitation.

Regular vulnerability scanning and assessment are essential components of an effective cybersecurity strategy. By continuously monitoring and identifying vulnerable services, you can proactively protect your network from potential threats and stay ahead of attackers.

It's worth noting that identifying vulnerable services is not a one-time task but an ongoing process. New vulnerabilities are discovered regularly, and services may change over time. Therefore, regular vulnerability assessments, periodic scans, and keeping software and systems up to date are essential practices for maintaining a secure network environment.

In summary, identifying vulnerable services is a crucial aspect of network security assessments. NMAP provides techniques such as version detection and NSE scripts to help pinpoint vulnerable services within your network. When assessing vulnerabilities, consider factors such as severity, CVSS scores, and potential impact to prioritize remediation efforts. Regular vulnerability scanning and proactive measures are essential for maintaining a secure network and protecting against emerging threats.

Assessing network weaknesses is a critical step in enhancing the security of your organization's IT infrastructure. In a constantly evolving threat landscape, understanding and addressing vulnerabilities and weaknesses in your network is essential to prevent security breaches and data breaches.

Network weaknesses can manifest in various forms, ranging from misconfigured devices and unpatched software to outdated security policies and insufficient monitoring. To effectively assess and mitigate these weaknesses, organizations often employ a combination of tools, methodologies, and best practices.

One common approach to identifying network weaknesses is through vulnerability scanning. Vulnerability scanners, such as Nessus, OpenVAS, and Qualys, are specialized tools designed to scan networks for known vulnerabilities in software, configurations, and devices.

To conduct a vulnerability scan, you can use a tool like Nessus by running a command like this:

```
nessus -q -T html --plugin-set=all --scan --targets=[Target]
```

In this command, "[Target]" represents the network or IP addresses you want to scan. Nessus will perform an automated scan, identify vulnerabilities, and provide a detailed report highlighting the weaknesses found.

Vulnerability scanning tools use extensive databases of known vulnerabilities, such as the National Vulnerability Database (NVD), to compare the configuration and software versions of scanned devices against known security issues.

Upon completion of the scan, you will receive a report that categorizes vulnerabilities based on their severity, provides detailed descriptions, and offers recommendations for remediation. This report is a valuable resource for prioritizing and addressing network weaknesses.

Another method for assessing network weaknesses is through penetration testing. Penetration testing, often referred to as "pen testing," involves simulating cyberattacks on a network to identify vulnerabilities and weaknesses that could be exploited by malicious actors.

Penetration testers, also known as ethical hackers, use a variety of techniques and tools to assess network security. These tests can include external and internal assessments, web application testing, and social engineering exercises.

To conduct a penetration test, organizations often hire experienced penetration testers or engage third-party security firms. These experts use tools like Metasploit, Burp Suite, and custom scripts to identify vulnerabilities and demonstrate potential exploitation scenarios.

During a penetration test, testers attempt to exploit weaknesses to gain unauthorized access, escalate privileges, and compromise systems. The results of a penetration test provide organizations with a realistic understanding of their network's security posture and potential vulnerabilities.

In addition to automated tools and penetration testing, organizations can assess network weaknesses by reviewing and improving their security policies and procedures. Strong security policies outline guidelines for network configurations, access controls, data handling, and incident response.

Security policies should be periodically reviewed and updated to address emerging threats and vulnerabilities. This process ensures that policies remain relevant and effective in safeguarding the network.

Another essential aspect of assessing network weaknesses is monitoring and log analysis. Security Information and Event Management (SIEM) solutions, such as Splunk and ELK Stack, help organizations collect, analyze, and correlate log data from various sources, including network devices, servers, and applications.

By continuously monitoring network traffic and system logs, organizations can identify unusual or suspicious activities that may indicate weaknesses or security breaches. Incident detection and response play a crucial role in addressing network weaknesses promptly.

To deploy a SIEM solution, organizations need to configure log sources, define alert rules, and establish incident response procedures. By centralizing log data and automating threat detection, SIEM solutions enable organizations to proactively identify and mitigate network weaknesses.

Another effective method for assessing network weaknesses is the use of threat modeling. Threat modeling is a proactive approach that involves identifying potential threats, vulnerabilities, and weaknesses in a network before they can be exploited.

To perform threat modeling, organizations can follow these steps:

Identify assets: Determine what assets are valuable or critical to your organization, such as servers, databases, and sensitive data.

Identify threats: Identify potential threats, including external attackers, insider threats, malware, and natural disasters.

Identify vulnerabilities: Analyze the network architecture, software, and configurations to identify potential weaknesses and vulnerabilities.

Assess risks: Evaluate the likelihood and impact of potential threats exploiting identified vulnerabilities. Mitigate risks: Develop and implement security controls and measures to reduce or mitigate identified risks. Monitor and update: Continuously monitor the network for changes, emerging threats, and evolving weaknesses, and update your threat model accordingly.

By systematically assessing network weaknesses through threat modeling, organizations can proactively strengthen their security posture and reduce the risk of exploitation.

Additionally, organizations can leverage continuous security testing techniques, such as automated vulnerability scanning, security code reviews, and configuration assessments. These techniques help identify and address weaknesses in an ongoing and proactive manner, minimizing the window of opportunity for attackers.

In summary, assessing network weaknesses is a fundamental aspect of network security. Methods for identifying weaknesses include vulnerability scanning, penetration testing, security policy reviews, monitoring and log analysis, threat modeling, and continuous security testing. By regularly assessing and addressing network weaknesses, organizations can enhance their security posture and reduce the risk of security breaches and data compromises.

Chapter 10: Best Practices for Secure Network Scanning

Secure scanning practices are essential for conducting network scans without inadvertently introducing security risks or disruptions. Network scanning, a valuable tool for assessing network security and vulnerabilities, must be performed with caution and consideration for the potential impact on the target systems and the network as a whole.

One of the primary considerations in secure scanning practices is obtaining proper authorization. Before conducting any network scans, it is crucial to gain explicit permission from the owner or administrator of the target network or systems. Unauthorized scanning can be interpreted as a hostile act and may result in legal consequences or damage to relationships between organizations.

To obtain authorization, organizations should establish clear communication channels with their counterparts and follow the established procedures for requesting permission to scan. This typically involves defining the scope of the scan, including the IP addresses, ports, and services to be scanned, as well as the timeframe during which the scan will occur.

Once authorization is obtained, it is essential to plan the scan carefully. This involves selecting the appropriate scanning tools, techniques, and parameters based on the goals of the scan and the scope defined in the authorization.

Many scanning tools, including NMAP, offer a wide range of options for customization. For example, you can specify the type of scan (e.g., TCP Connect Scan, SYN Scan), scan timing, and the list of target hosts or IP ranges.

To initiate a secure network scan using NMAP, you can use a command like the following:

```
nmap -sS -T4 -p 1-1000 [Target]
```
In this command, "-sS" specifies a SYN Scan, "-T4" sets the scan timing to "Aggressive," and "-p 1-1000" scans ports in the range of 1 to 1000. Replace "[Target]" with the target IP address or hostname.

Careful planning also includes considering the potential impact of the scan on the target systems. Scans can sometimes disrupt or overload systems, especially if they are intensive or involve probing a large number of ports. Organizations should conduct scans during off-peak hours when possible and be prepared to abort the scan if any adverse effects are observed.

Another crucial aspect of secure scanning practices is ensuring data integrity and confidentiality. During a scan, sensitive information may be exchanged between the scanning tool and the target systems. To protect this data, it is advisable to use encryption, such as SSH or SSL, when communicating with remote systems.

For example, when using NMAP to scan a target system via SSH, you can specify the SSH key and port using the following command:

```
nmap -p [SSH Port] --script ssh-hostkey --script-args
ssh_hostkey=[SSH Key] [Target]
```
This command uses the "--script" option to run an NSE script for SSH host key checking and specifies the SSH port and key with "--script-args."

Furthermore, it is essential to handle scan results securely. Scan reports often contain sensitive information about the target network's configuration and vulnerabilities. To protect these reports, organizations should restrict access to authorized personnel only and encrypt them when storing or transmitting.

Access control mechanisms, such as file permissions and user authentication, should be in place to prevent unauthorized access to scan reports. Encrypting reports using strong encryption algorithms and secure transmission protocols ensures that the information remains confidential.

Additionally, organizations should define retention and disposal policies for scan reports to manage data lifecycle effectively. Old or outdated reports may contain information that is no longer relevant and could pose a security risk if retained unnecessarily.

Another important aspect of secure scanning practices is compliance with laws and regulations. Depending on the organization's location and the target network's jurisdiction, there may be legal requirements and privacy regulations that govern scanning activities.

Organizations should be aware of relevant laws, such as data protection and privacy regulations, and ensure that their scanning practices comply with these legal requirements. Failure to comply with legal obligations can result in severe penalties and legal consequences.

Moreover, ethical considerations play a significant role in secure scanning practices. Ethical hackers and security professionals must adhere to a code of conduct that emphasizes responsible and lawful behavior. Respecting the privacy and confidentiality of target networks and systems is essential.

To maintain ethical standards, organizations should establish clear guidelines and policies for their security teams and provide training on ethical scanning practices. Furthermore, organizations should engage in responsible disclosure when they discover vulnerabilities during scans, allowing the target organization to address the issues before public disclosure.

In summary, secure scanning practices are essential for conducting network scans in a responsible and ethical manner. Key considerations include obtaining proper authorization, careful planning, data protection, compliance with laws and regulations, and adherence to ethical guidelines. By following secure scanning practices, organizations can assess network security and vulnerabilities while minimizing potential risks and maintaining ethical standards.

Legal and ethical considerations are paramount in the field of network scanning and cybersecurity. As organizations and individuals engage in activities such as vulnerability scanning, penetration testing, and network reconnaissance, it is essential to understand and adhere to the legal and ethical boundaries that govern these practices.

One of the foundational principles of legal and ethical considerations in cybersecurity is obtaining proper authorization. Unauthorized access to computer systems and networks is a violation of laws in many jurisdictions and can result in criminal charges, penalties, and civil lawsuits.

To ensure compliance with the law, organizations and individuals must obtain explicit permission from the owner or administrator of the target network or system before conducting any scanning or testing activities. This authorization typically involves defining the scope and duration of the activities, as well as any limitations or restrictions.

Failure to obtain proper authorization can have serious legal consequences and can damage relationships between organizations or individuals.

In addition to authorization, ethical considerations play a crucial role in cybersecurity practices. Ethical behavior involves adhering to a code of conduct that emphasizes honesty, integrity, and responsible behavior.

Ethical hackers and security professionals are expected to conduct their activities with the utmost respect for the privacy and confidentiality of target networks and systems. This includes protecting sensitive data, avoiding data breaches, and refraining from causing harm or disruption.

When identifying vulnerabilities or weaknesses during scanning or testing, responsible disclosure is an ethical practice. This means that if security professionals discover vulnerabilities, they should promptly notify the owner or administrator of the affected systems and provide them with the necessary information to address the issues.

Ethical hackers should refrain from exploiting vulnerabilities for personal gain or malicious purposes and should instead assist organizations in improving their security posture.

Legal and ethical considerations also extend to the use of scanning tools and techniques. Many scanning tools, including NMAP, offer a wide range of capabilities for network reconnaissance and vulnerability assessment. However, the use of these tools must comply with the law and ethical standards.

To deploy scanning tools ethically and legally, it is essential to follow best practices. This includes obtaining proper training in the use of these tools, understanding their capabilities and limitations, and using them only for legitimate and authorized purposes.

Additionally, organizations and individuals should be aware of laws and regulations that apply to cybersecurity activities. Laws related to computer crime, data protection, and privacy can vary significantly between jurisdictions, and ignorance of the law is not a valid defense in legal proceedings.

To ensure legal compliance, organizations should consult with legal experts who specialize in cybersecurity and privacy laws. Legal professionals can provide guidance on how to conduct scanning and testing activities while adhering to the law.

Furthermore, organizations and individuals should keep abreast of changes in laws and regulations that may impact cybersecurity practices. Legislation related to cybersecurity is continually evolving to address new threats and challenges.

For example, the General Data Protection Regulation (GDPR) in the European Union introduced strict requirements for the protection of personal data and imposed significant penalties for data breaches. Compliance with GDPR and similar regulations is essential for organizations that handle personal data.

Another important legal consideration is the use of third-party scanning services. When engaging external vendors or consultants to conduct scanning or testing activities, organizations must ensure that the services provided comply with legal and ethical standards.

Contracts and agreements with third-party vendors should clearly outline the scope of work, authorization requirements, and expectations for compliance with laws and regulations. Additionally, organizations should conduct due diligence to verify the reputation and ethical standards of the vendors they engage.

In summary, legal and ethical considerations are fundamental principles in the field of cybersecurity and network scanning. Obtaining proper authorization, adhering to ethical guidelines, and complying with laws and regulations are essential for responsible and lawful cybersecurity practices.

Legal and ethical considerations also extend to the use of scanning tools and techniques, the responsible disclosure of vulnerabilities, and the engagement of third-party vendors. To navigate the complex landscape of cybersecurity laws and regulations, organizations should seek legal counsel and stay informed about legal developments in the field.

By upholding legal and ethical standards, organizations and individuals can conduct network scanning and cybersecurity activities responsibly, protect data and privacy, and contribute to a more secure digital environment.

BOOK 2
NMAP MASTERY
ADVANCED TECHNIQUES AND STRATEGIES FOR NETWORK
ANALYSIS

ROB BOTWRIGHT

Chapter 1: Advanced NMAP Scanning Methods

Scan optimization techniques are essential for improving the efficiency and effectiveness of network scanning activities. Network scanning plays a crucial role in assessing security vulnerabilities, identifying weaknesses, and ensuring the overall security of an organization's IT infrastructure.

Optimizing scans involves refining scanning processes to achieve desired outcomes while minimizing resource consumption and potential disruption to the target network. By employing scan optimization techniques, organizations can conduct scans more efficiently and obtain actionable results.

One fundamental aspect of scan optimization is understanding the scope of the scan. Before initiating a scan, it is crucial to define clear objectives and determine the specific targets, such as IP addresses, subnets, or network ranges, to be included in the scan.

Understanding the scope helps in focusing scanning efforts on critical assets and areas of interest. It also reduces unnecessary scanning of irrelevant or low-priority systems, saving time and resources.

To specify the target hosts or IP addresses in a scan using NMAP, you can provide them as arguments in the command:

nmap [Target1] [Target2] ...

For example, to scan two target hosts, you can use:

nmap 192.168.1.1 192.168.1.2

NMAP will concentrate scanning efforts on the provided targets, optimizing the scan for specific areas of interest.

Scan timing is another crucial factor in scan optimization. The timing of scans can impact network performance, as well as the accuracy of scan results. Adjusting the scan timing can help strike a balance between thoroughness and resource consumption.

NMAP provides timing options to control the pace of a scan. For example, the "-T" option allows you to specify the scan timing template, which ranges from "Paranoid" (slow and stealthy) to "Insane" (fast and aggressive).

To use the "Aggressive" timing template in an NMAP scan, you can include the "-T4" option:

nmap -T4 [Target]

This setting optimizes the scan for faster results without being overly aggressive and potentially causing disruptions.

In addition to timing, scan optimization involves selecting appropriate scanning techniques. NMAP offers various scan types, such as SYN scans, ACK scans, and comprehensive scans like the "-A" option for OS detection and service enumeration.

Choosing the right scan type depends on the objectives of the scan. For example, if the goal is to perform a quick discovery of open ports, a SYN scan (-sS) may be suitable:

nmap -sS [Target]

On the other hand, if you need detailed information about services and operating systems, a comprehensive scan with the "-A" option can be used:

nmap -A [Target]

Using the most appropriate scan techniques optimizes the scan for specific goals and reduces unnecessary overhead. Furthermore, scan optimization includes the consideration of scan options and parameters. NMAP offers a multitude of options that allow users to fine-tune the scan according to their needs.

For example, the "-p" option allows you to specify the range of ports to scan. You can optimize the scan by narrowing down the port range to focus on specific services:

nmap -p 80,443 [Target]

This command scans only ports 80 (HTTP) and 443 (HTTPS) on the target, optimizing the scan for web services.

Another optimization technique is the use of scan scripts provided by the NMAP Scripting Engine (NSE). NSE scripts allow users to automate specific tasks during a scan, such as service identification, vulnerability detection, and information gathering.

To run NSE scripts during a scan, you can use the "--script" or "-sC" option:

nmap --script [Script] [Target]

For example, to perform a scan with scripts that detect vulnerabilities related to HTTP, you can use:

nmap --script http-vuln* [Target]

This command optimizes the scan by automating the vulnerability assessment process.

Scan optimization also involves managing scan results effectively. Once the scan is complete, it is crucial to analyze the results efficiently and prioritize action items based on the findings.

Organizations can optimize their response to scan results by categorizing vulnerabilities, assessing their severity, and defining remediation priorities. This optimization ensures that critical vulnerabilities are addressed promptly, minimizing the risk of exploitation.

Additionally, organizations can leverage automation and reporting tools to streamline the handling of scan results. Automated workflows can help assign tasks to relevant teams or individuals, track remediation progress, and ensure that vulnerabilities are addressed systematically.

Finally, scan optimization extends to ongoing scanning practices. Regular scans should be scheduled to monitor changes in the network environment and identify emerging vulnerabilities.

Scheduled scans can be optimized by adjusting scan frequencies, prioritizing critical systems, and aligning scanning activities with change management processes.

In summary, scan optimization techniques are essential for enhancing the efficiency and effectiveness of network scanning activities. Optimizing scans involves defining clear objectives, adjusting scan timing, selecting appropriate scan techniques, and fine-tuning scan options. Managing scan results efficiently and prioritizing remediation efforts based on severity are integral to scan optimization. Automation and reporting tools can further streamline the handling of scan results.

Ongoing scanning practices, aligned with organizational goals and change management processes, help maintain network security and ensure the timely identification of vulnerabilities.

By applying scan optimization techniques, organizations can maximize the benefits of network scanning while minimizing resource consumption and potential disruptions.

Advanced host discovery techniques are essential for comprehensive network reconnaissance and understanding the topology of a target network. Host discovery involves identifying live hosts and their associated services, which is a fundamental step in network scanning and vulnerability assessment.

While basic host discovery methods like ICMP ping and TCP ping scans are commonly used, advanced host discovery techniques provide a more in-depth and accurate view of the network.

One advanced host discovery technique is the use of the ARP (Address Resolution Protocol) scan. ARP is a protocol used in Ethernet networks to map IP addresses to MAC (Media Access Control) addresses. By sending ARP requests for a range of IP addresses, an attacker can determine which IP addresses are in use and map them to specific physical devices on the network.

To perform an ARP scan using NMAP, you can use the following command:

nmap -PR [Target]

In this command, "-PR" specifies an ARP ping scan, and "[Target]" represents the target network or IP range.

The ARP scan is particularly useful in scenarios where ICMP or TCP ping scans may be blocked or filtered by firewalls or security devices. It can reveal live hosts that might otherwise go unnoticed.

Another advanced host discovery technique involves using reverse DNS (Domain Name System) lookups. DNS is a critical protocol that maps human-readable domain names to IP addresses. Reverse DNS lookup does the opposite: it resolves IP addresses back to domain names.

To perform a reverse DNS lookup using NMAP, you can include the "-R" option in your scan command:

nmap -R [Target]

By performing reverse DNS lookups on discovered IP addresses, you can obtain information about the hostnames associated with live hosts. This can be valuable for identifying the purpose or ownership of devices on the network.

Additionally, NMAP offers the option to use brute-force host discovery techniques. These techniques involve sending a large number of packets to a range of IP addresses in an attempt to identify live hosts.

One example is the "ACK ping" scan, which sends TCP ACK (Acknowledgment) packets to a range of ports on target hosts. The goal is to elicit responses from live hosts that reveal their presence.

To perform an ACK ping scan using NMAP, you can use the following command:

nmap -PA [Target]

The "-PA" option specifies an ACK ping scan.

It's important to note that brute-force host discovery techniques can be more resource-intensive and potentially disruptive to the network than other methods.

Organizations should use them cautiously and consider their impact on network performance.

Additionally, advanced host discovery techniques can benefit from the use of NMAP's built-in script engine, the NSE (NMAP Scripting Engine). NSE scripts can automate various host discovery tasks and provide additional information about discovered hosts.

For example, the "dns-ip6-arpa-scan" script in NMAP can be used to perform reverse DNS lookups for IPv6 addresses. This script automates the process of resolving IPv6 addresses to domain names.

To run the "dns-ip6-arpa-scan" script in NMAP, you can use the following command:

nmap --script dns-ip6-arpa-scan [Target]

The script will perform reverse DNS lookups for IPv6 addresses discovered during the scan.

In addition to ARP scans, reverse DNS lookups, and brute-force techniques, advanced host discovery can also involve analyzing network traffic. Packet capturing and analysis tools like Wireshark can be used to monitor network traffic and identify live hosts based on their communication patterns.

By capturing network traffic and examining packet headers, it is possible to detect live hosts even if they do not respond to traditional ping scans.

While advanced host discovery techniques offer more comprehensive insights into a network's topology, they should be used judiciously and with proper authorization. Indiscriminate scanning or probing of hosts can be perceived as malicious and may lead to unwanted consequences.

Furthermore, organizations should consider privacy and data protection concerns when performing host discovery. Reverse DNS lookups, in particular, may reveal sensitive information about hosts, such as domain names associated with internal systems.

In summary, advanced host discovery techniques are valuable tools for gaining a deeper understanding of a target network's live hosts and their associated services. These techniques, including ARP scans, reverse DNS lookups, brute-force methods, and traffic analysis, can provide a more comprehensive view of the network topology.

Organizations and security professionals should use these techniques responsibly, obtain proper authorization, and be mindful of potential impacts on network performance and privacy.

By leveraging advanced host discovery techniques, security professionals can enhance their network reconnaissance efforts and better prepare for subsequent scanning and vulnerability assessment tasks.

Chapter 2: Deep Dive into NMAP Scripting

Creating custom NSE (NMAP Scripting Engine) scripts is a powerful capability that allows security professionals to extend the functionality of NMAP and tailor it to their specific needs. NSE scripts are written in the Lua programming language and can automate various tasks during network scanning and reconnaissance.

One of the primary advantages of creating custom NSE scripts is the ability to automate repetitive tasks. By defining specific tasks and behaviors in a script, security professionals can save time and ensure consistency in their scanning and testing processes.

To create a custom NSE script, it's essential to have a basic understanding of the Lua programming language. Lua is a lightweight and versatile scripting language known for its simplicity and ease of integration with other applications.

Before diving into script development, you should have NMAP installed on your system. You can check if NMAP is installed by running the following command:

nmap --version

If NMAP is not installed, you can download and install it from the official NMAP website.

To begin creating a custom NSE script, you need to choose a specific task or functionality that you want to automate or enhance within NMAP. For example, you may want to create a script that identifies vulnerable web servers based on specific patterns in HTTP responses.

Once you have identified the task, you can start writing your script. NSE scripts are typically stored in the "scripts" directory within the NMAP installation directory.

To create a custom script, you can use a text editor or an integrated development environment (IDE) that supports Lua scripting. Let's assume you're using a text editor to create a script called "vuln-web-servers.nse."

Here's an example of a simple NSE script that checks for vulnerable web servers based on specific HTTP responses:

lua

-- NSE script to identify vulnerable web servers -- This script sends an HTTP request to the target and checks for specific patterns in the response. -- Usage: nmap -p 80 --script vuln-web-servers.nse [Target] portrule = function(host, port) return port.number == 80 end action = function(host, port) local http_req = "GET / HTTP/1.1\r\nHost: " .. host.ip .. "\r\n\r\n" local response = http.get(host, port, http_req) if response.status == 200 and string.match(response.body, "vulnerable_pattern") then return "Found a vulnerable web server on port " .. port.number else return "No vulnerable web server found on port " .. port.number end end

In this script, we define a "portrule" function that specifies that the script should only run on port 80. The "action" function sends an HTTP request to the target and checks the response for a specific pattern that indicates vulnerability.

Once you've created your custom NSE script, you need to place it in the "scripts" directory within the NMAP installation directory.

To run your custom script, you can use the following NMAP command:

nmap -p 80 --script vuln-web-servers.nse [Target]

Replace "[Target]" with the IP address or hostname of the target system you want to scan.

81

When the scan is complete, NMAP will execute your custom script and display the results in the terminal.

Creating custom NSE scripts allows you to tailor NMAP to your specific requirements and automate tasks that are unique to your organization or testing objectives.

Moreover, NSE scripts can be shared with the security community, contributing to the growing library of scripts available for NMAP users worldwide.

To share your custom script or access scripts created by others, you can visit the official NMAP NSE script repository or participate in forums and communities dedicated to NMAP scripting and network security.

When developing custom NSE scripts, it's important to follow best practices to ensure the reliability and effectiveness of your scripts.

First, thoroughly test your scripts in a controlled environment before using them in a production or live network. Testing helps identify and address any errors, issues, or unexpected behaviors in your script.

Additionally, consider adding error handling and validation checks to your scripts to handle various scenarios gracefully. This can help prevent script failures or unintended consequences during scans.

Documenting your custom NSE scripts is also essential. Include comments within your script to explain its purpose, usage, and any specific requirements or dependencies.

This documentation makes it easier for others to understand and use your script, and it can serve as a reference for yourself in the future.

Furthermore, keep your scripts up to date. Regularly review and update your scripts to ensure they remain compatible with the latest versions of NMAP and any changes in network protocols or technologies.

Finally, consider contributing your custom scripts to the NMAP community. Sharing your scripts can benefit other security professionals and help improve the overall capabilities of NMAP.

In summary, creating custom NSE scripts for NMAP allows security professionals to automate tasks, enhance scanning capabilities, and tailor NMAP to their specific needs. Script development involves choosing a task, writing Lua code, and placing the script in the appropriate directory within the NMAP installation.

Testing, documentation, and script maintenance are crucial aspects of script development. Sharing your custom scripts with the security community can contribute to the collective knowledge and effectiveness of NMAP users worldwide.

By harnessing the power of custom NSE scripts, security professionals can conduct more efficient and targeted network reconnaissance and vulnerability assessment.

Scripting for specific scenarios is a valuable skill for security professionals who want to tailor their network scanning and reconnaissance efforts to address unique challenges and requirements. While NMAP's built-in scripts provide a wide range of functionality, there are situations where custom scripts are necessary to achieve specific goals.

One common scenario where scripting is essential is when dealing with complex or proprietary protocols. In many networks, especially in enterprise environments, there are custom applications and protocols that NMAP's standard scripts may not fully understand or interact with.

For example, consider a network that uses a proprietary authentication protocol for access control. In such cases, security professionals can create custom NSE scripts to emulate the protocol's behavior and test for vulnerabilities or misconfigurations.

Developing custom scripts for proprietary protocols requires a deep understanding of the protocol's specifications, message formats, and expected responses. Security professionals need to reverse-engineer the protocol to craft scripts that can interact with the target system effectively.

Here's an example of a simplified custom NSE script that emulates a basic authentication request for a proprietary protocol:

lua

```
-- Custom NSE script for emulating a proprietary authentication protocol portrule = function(host, port) return port.number == 1234 -- Replace with the actual port number end action = function(host, port) local socket = nmap.new_socket() local result = {} -- Craft the authentication request packet local request_packet = "\x01\x02\x03\x04" -- Replace with the actual request packet format -- Send the request packet to the target socket:connect(host.ip, port.number) socket:send(request_packet) -- Receive and analyze the response from the target local response = socket:receive() if response == "\x05\x06\x07\x08" then table.insert(result, "Authentication successful") else table.insert(result, "Authentication failed") end socket:close() return table.concat(result, "\n") end
```

In this script, we define a custom port rule to specify the port on which the proprietary protocol operates. The "action" function emulates an authentication request, sends it to the target system, and analyzes the response to determine whether the authentication was successful.

Another scenario where scripting for specific scenarios is valuable is in the context of IoT (Internet of Things) security. IoT devices often use non-standard communication protocols, making them challenging to assess using standard NMAP scripts.

Security professionals may need to develop custom scripts to interact with IoT devices, identify vulnerabilities, and assess their security posture.

For instance, consider a network that includes IoT devices using a proprietary communication protocol for device management. A custom NSE script can be created to establish communication with these devices and assess their security configuration.

Developing custom scripts for IoT devices may involve analyzing device firmware, capturing network traffic between the device and its management server, and reverse-engineering the device's communication protocol.

Here's a simplified example of a custom NSE script for interacting with an IoT device using a proprietary protocol:

lua

```
-- Custom NSE script for interacting with an IoT device
portrule = function(host, port) return port.number == 12345 -- Replace with the actual port number end action = function(host, port) local socket = nmap.new_socket() local result = {} -- Establish communication with the IoT device socket:connect(host.ip, port.number) -- Send a command to retrieve device information local command = "GET /device_info" socket:send(command .. "\n") -- Receive and analyze the device's response local response = socket:receive() if string.match(response, "Device Model: ABC123") then table.insert(result, "Device identified as Model ABC123") else table.insert(result, "Device model identification failed") end -- Close the socket socket:close() return table.concat(result, "\n") end
```

In this script, we define a custom port rule to specify the port associated with the IoT device's management interface. The "action" function sends a command to retrieve device information, receives the response, and analyzes it to identify the device's model.

Scripting for specific scenarios often requires a deep understanding of the target systems, protocols, and the desired security objectives. It may involve research, reverse engineering, and experimentation to develop effective scripts.

When developing custom scripts for specific scenarios, it's essential to follow best practices to ensure script reliability and maintainability.

First and foremost, thoroughly test your scripts in a controlled environment to verify their functionality and correctness. Testing helps identify any issues or unexpected behavior in your scripts.

Additionally, consider error handling and validation checks to ensure that your scripts gracefully handle various scenarios, including unexpected responses or errors from the target systems.

Documentation is crucial for custom scripts created for specific scenarios. Include comments within your script to explain its purpose, usage, and any specific requirements or dependencies.

Documenting your scripts makes it easier for others to understand and use them, and it serves as a reference for yourself in the future.

Regularly review and update your custom scripts to ensure compatibility with the latest versions of NMAP, changes in network protocols, or updates to target systems.

Lastly, consider sharing your custom scripts with the security community. Contributing your scripts to repositories or forums dedicated to NMAP scripting and network security can benefit other security professionals and foster collaboration in addressing specific scenarios.

In summary, scripting for specific scenarios is a valuable skill for security professionals, enabling them to tailor their network scanning and reconnaissance efforts to unique challenges and requirements. Custom NSE scripts can be developed to interact with complex or proprietary protocols, assess IoT device security, and address specific security objectives.

When creating custom scripts, follow best practices, including thorough testing, error handling, documentation, and regular updates. Sharing your custom scripts with the security community can contribute to collective knowledge and effectiveness in addressing specific scenarios effectively and efficiently.

Chapter 3: OS Fingerprinting and Identification

Identifying OS signatures is a critical aspect of network reconnaissance and security assessment, as it allows security professionals to determine the operating systems running on target devices. Understanding the OS signatures of devices on a network is essential for vulnerability assessment, security hardening, and overall network security.

NMAP, a popular open-source network scanning tool, provides capabilities for identifying OS signatures through a technique known as OS fingerprinting. OS fingerprinting is the process of analyzing specific network behavior and responses to distinguish one operating system from another. NMAP employs various methods of OS fingerprinting to achieve accurate results. One of the most commonly used OS fingerprinting techniques in NMAP is the TCP/IP fingerprinting method, which analyzes how a device responds to different TCP/IP packet sequences.

To perform OS fingerprinting using NMAP, you can use the following command:

nmap -O [Target]

Replace "[Target]" with the IP address or hostname of the target system you want to scan.

NMAP will send a series of specially crafted TCP/IP packets to the target and analyze the responses to make an educated guess about the operating system. This guess is based on patterns, quirks, and unique characteristics of how different operating systems handle network traffic.

The accuracy of OS fingerprinting largely depends on the number of responses NMAP receives and the quality of the collected data. To improve accuracy, NMAP may send multiple probes to gather more information and refine the OS guess.

Another method of OS fingerprinting used by NMAP is the use of the Remote OS Detection (RD) script. The RD script goes beyond TCP/IP fingerprinting and takes into account additional network behaviors and characteristics, such as initial TTL (Time To Live) values, IP ID sequences, and more.

To use the RD script for OS detection in NMAP, you can include the "-A" option in your scan command:

nmap -A [Target]

The "-A" option enables OS detection along with service and version detection, providing a more comprehensive view of the target system.

NMAP's OS fingerprinting capabilities are continuously updated and refined to keep up with changes in network technologies and operating systems. NMAP maintains a database of known OS fingerprints, and these fingerprints are regularly updated and expanded to ensure accurate identification.

However, there are challenges and limitations associated with OS fingerprinting. One limitation is that some devices and firewalls may intentionally provide misleading responses to confuse OS fingerprinting techniques. This can make it challenging to accurately identify the operating system in such cases.

Additionally, virtualization and containerization technologies can introduce complexities in OS fingerprinting. Virtual machines and containers may share a common OS kernel, making it difficult to distinguish between them based on network behavior alone.

In situations where OS fingerprinting using NMAP may not yield accurate results, security professionals can consider alternative methods. Passive OS fingerprinting is one such method, where the operating system is inferred based on observed network traffic patterns and behaviors over time.

Passive OS fingerprinting does not involve sending specific probes to the target system but relies on the analysis of network packets and characteristics.

Another approach to OS identification is using dedicated OS detection tools and libraries that specialize in this task. These tools often provide more detailed and accurate results, especially when dealing with complex or specialized operating systems.

In addition to OS fingerprinting, NMAP offers other features and options that can enhance network reconnaissance and security assessment. These include service detection, version detection, and vulnerability scanning.

Service detection involves identifying the services running on open ports of a target system. NMAP can provide information about the type of service, such as HTTP, SSH, or FTP, running on a specific port.

To perform service detection using NMAP, you can use the following command:

nmap -sV [Target]

Replace "[Target]" with the IP address or hostname of the target system.

Version detection takes service detection a step further by attempting to determine the exact version or software release of the identified service.

To enable version detection in NMAP, you can include the "-sV" option in your scan command, as shown above.

Vulnerability scanning involves using NMAP scripts and plugins to identify known vulnerabilities in the target system. NMAP provides a wide range of scripts and plugins for vulnerability assessment, covering various services and applications.

To perform vulnerability scanning with NMAP, you can use the following command:

nmap --script vuln [Target]

Replace "[Target]" with the IP address or hostname of the target system.

In summary, identifying OS signatures is a critical part of network reconnaissance and security assessment, enabling security professionals to determine the operating systems running on target devices. NMAP offers robust OS fingerprinting capabilities through TCP/IP fingerprinting and the Remote OS Detection (RD) script, helping users accurately identify operating systems.

While OS fingerprinting provides valuable information, it has limitations and may not always yield accurate results. Consider alternative methods, such as passive OS fingerprinting or dedicated OS detection tools, when faced with challenging scenarios.

NMAP also offers additional features, including service detection, version detection, and vulnerability scanning, to enhance network reconnaissance and security assessment efforts. These features, when used effectively, contribute to a more comprehensive understanding of the target network and its security posture.

Bypassing OS detection evasion is a topic that falls within the realm of network security and penetration testing. While identifying the operating system (OS) of a target system is a fundamental part of network reconnaissance, there are situations where an attacker or security tester may want to hide or manipulate the OS fingerprint of a device to evade detection.

Network security professionals and ethical hackers often use tools like NMAP, which is renowned for its OS fingerprinting capabilities, to assess the security posture of target networks. However, network defenders and system administrators are constantly improving their security measures, and one such measure is attempting to thwart OS detection techniques.

OS detection evasion typically involves altering network behaviors and responses to make a device's operating system appear different from what it actually is. This can confuse network scanning tools like NMAP, making it challenging to accurately identify the OS.

To bypass OS detection evasion, it's essential to understand some of the common evasion techniques used by system administrators and defenders.

One common technique used to thwart OS detection is called "OS fingerprint masking." In this technique, the defender configures the network stack or firewall to respond to network probes with generic or misleading responses that do not accurately represent the underlying OS.

For example, a network defender may configure a firewall to respond to certain TCP/IP packets with responses characteristic of a different OS. When NMAP sends probing packets, it receives responses that do not match the expected behavior of the actual OS, making OS detection more challenging.

Another evasion technique involves "packet scrubbing." Packet scrubbing is the process of modifying or removing specific information from network packets to disrupt OS fingerprinting.

For instance, a defender may alter the TTL (Time To Live) values of packets, fragment packets in unusual ways, or modify IP ID sequences to make it difficult for NMAP to identify the OS based on packet analysis.

These techniques are designed to introduce inconsistencies and anomalies in network responses, making it challenging for NMAP and similar tools to draw accurate conclusions about the OS.

In response to OS detection evasion techniques, NMAP and other network scanning tools continually update and refine their OS fingerprinting methods. This ongoing development helps improve accuracy and adapt to changes in network behaviors.

Security professionals and ethical hackers must be aware of these evasion techniques and employ strategies to bypass them effectively.

One approach to bypassing OS detection evasion is to use advanced OS fingerprinting techniques. NMAP, for example, offers more sophisticated fingerprinting methods, such as the Remote OS Detection (RD) script, which analyzes a broader range of network behaviors and characteristics.

By using advanced fingerprinting techniques like RD, security professionals can gather more data points to build a more accurate OS fingerprint and mitigate the effects of evasion techniques.

To use the RD script for OS detection in NMAP, you can include the "-A" option in your scan command, as mentioned earlier:

nmap -A [Target]

The "-A" option enables OS detection along with service and version detection, providing a more comprehensive view of the target system.

Another strategy for bypassing OS detection evasion is to use passive OS fingerprinting techniques. Passive OS fingerprinting involves observing network traffic patterns and behaviors over time to infer the OS without actively sending probing packets.

While passive OS fingerprinting may not be as precise as active methods, it can be effective in situations where evasion techniques disrupt active probing.

Security professionals can use network monitoring and packet capture tools like Wireshark to passively analyze network traffic and identify OS characteristics.

Additionally, security testers can use specialized OS detection tools and libraries that are designed to bypass evasion techniques. These tools often employ advanced algorithms and heuristics to infer OS information accurately, even in the presence of evasion measures.

When employing OS detection evasion techniques, security professionals should exercise caution and adhere to ethical guidelines. Evasion techniques should only be used in authorized and controlled environments, such as penetration testing scenarios, where the goal is to assess network security and identify vulnerabilities.

It is crucial to obtain proper authorization and informed consent from network owners and stakeholders before conducting any OS detection evasion activities.

Furthermore, it is essential to document and report any evasion techniques used during security assessments and penetration tests. Transparent communication with the organization being tested ensures that the findings are properly understood and can lead to necessary security improvements.

In summary, bypassing OS detection evasion is a challenging but essential aspect of network reconnaissance and security assessment. Defenders and system administrators employ various techniques to mask or alter OS fingerprints to thwart network scanning tools like NMAP.

Security professionals and ethical hackers must be aware of these evasion techniques and employ advanced OS fingerprinting methods, passive techniques, and specialized tools to bypass evasion effectively.

While evasion techniques can be valuable for assessing network security, they should only be used in authorized and controlled environments with proper authorization and ethical considerations in mind.

By staying informed about evasion techniques and employing effective strategies, security professionals can enhance their ability to accurately assess network security and identify vulnerabilities.

Chapter 4: Advanced Service Enumeration

Service fingerprinting techniques are crucial for network reconnaissance and security assessment, as they allow security professionals to identify and understand the services running on target systems. Knowing the specific services and their versions is essential for vulnerability assessment, patch management, and overall network security.

Service fingerprinting involves the process of determining the type and version of services running on open ports of a target system. These services can range from web servers and databases to email servers and remote access services.

NMAP, a popular open-source network scanning tool, provides robust capabilities for service fingerprinting. It achieves service fingerprinting by analyzing how target systems respond to specific probes and requests sent by NMAP.

One of the primary methods used by NMAP for service fingerprinting is banner grabbing. Banner grabbing involves sending requests or probes to open ports and analyzing the banners or responses received from the services.

To perform banner grabbing using NMAP, you can use the following command:

nmap -sV [Target]
Replace "[Target]" with the IP address or hostname of the target system you want to scan.

NMAP will send probes to open ports and collect banners or responses from the services running on those ports. By analyzing the banners, NMAP can identify the type and version of the services.

For example, if NMAP receives a banner that mentions "Apache/2.4.29," it can determine that the target system is running an Apache web server version 2.4.29.

Banner grabbing is a straightforward and effective method for service fingerprinting, but it relies on the accuracy of the information provided in the banners. Service administrators may customize or obscure banners, making it challenging to obtain accurate results.

To address this limitation, NMAP offers version detection capabilities, which go beyond banner grabbing. Version detection involves sending additional probes and analyzing various aspects of service behavior to determine the exact version or software release.

To enable version detection in NMAP, you can include the "-sV" option in your scan command:

nmap -sV [Target]

The "-sV" option instructs NMAP to perform version detection in addition to service identification. This results in a more comprehensive view of the target services, including their specific versions.

Version detection in NMAP often involves sending probes that elicit unique responses from services. These probes may include sending specific requests, initiating a handshake, or querying specific attributes of the services.

For example, NMAP may send an HTTP request to a web server to retrieve the server's response headers. By analyzing the response headers, NMAP can determine not only that it's an Apache web server but also the precise version and configuration details.

Service fingerprinting techniques are not limited to NMAP alone. Other network scanning and reconnaissance tools and libraries offer similar capabilities for identifying services and their versions.

For example, Wireshark, a popular network protocol analyzer, can be used to capture and analyze network traffic to identify services based on their communication patterns and behavior.

Additionally, there are dedicated service fingerprinting tools and libraries, such as the "Service Detection Library" (libnmap), which can be integrated into custom scripts and applications to perform service identification.

When performing service fingerprinting, it's essential to consider the potential impact on the target systems. Sending probes and requests to open ports can generate traffic and logs on the target, which may be detected by network intrusion detection systems (IDS) or log monitoring solutions.

To minimize the impact and avoid unnecessary attention, security professionals can use techniques such as stealth scanning or slow scanning. These techniques involve adjusting the scanning speed, timing, and frequency to fly under the radar of network defenses.

For example, NMAP provides options like "--max-parallelism" and "--max-rate" to control the speed and rate of scanning, reducing the chances of triggering alarms.

In summary, service fingerprinting techniques are essential for network reconnaissance and security assessment, enabling security professionals to identify and understand the services running on target systems. NMAP, among other tools, provides banner grabbing and version detection capabilities to achieve accurate service identification.

Banner grabbing retrieves banners or responses from open ports, while version detection goes beyond banners to determine precise service versions.

Security professionals should be mindful of the potential impact of service fingerprinting on target systems and consider stealth scanning techniques to minimize detection.

By employing effective service fingerprinting techniques, security professionals can gain insights into network services, assess their security posture, and make informed decisions to enhance network security.

Detecting hidden services is a challenging and critical task in the field of network security and penetration testing, as hidden services may be used for legitimate purposes or for malicious activities. Hidden services are services that are intentionally configured to be less visible on a network, making them harder to detect and assess.

Security professionals and ethical hackers use various techniques and tools to uncover hidden services within a network. Detecting hidden services is crucial for understanding the complete network environment and identifying potential security risks.

One common technique for detecting hidden services is active scanning. Active scanning involves sending specific probes or requests to known ports to identify services that may not be visible through passive means.

For example, NMAP, a popular network scanning tool, can be used to perform active scanning to identify hidden services. To detect hidden services using NMAP, security professionals can use the following command:

nmap -p [Port Range] [Target]
Replace "[Port Range]" with the range of ports you want to scan (e.g., 1-65535) and "[Target]" with the IP address or hostname of the target system.
NMAP will send probes to the specified port range and report any services it detects. This method is effective for identifying services that may be configured to run on non-standard or less-visible ports.
Another technique for detecting hidden services is to analyze network traffic. Network traffic analysis involves capturing and inspecting network packets to identify unusual or suspicious patterns that may indicate the presence of hidden services.
Security professionals can use packet capture tools like Wireshark to capture and analyze network traffic. By examining packet payloads, headers, and communication patterns, they can uncover hidden services that may not be readily visible through standard port scanning.
Additionally, security professionals can employ intrusion detection systems (IDS) and network monitoring solutions to identify hidden services based on anomalous behavior or traffic patterns.
Passive DNS analysis is another valuable technique for detecting hidden services. DNS (Domain Name System) resolution data can provide insights into hidden services by revealing domain names or hostnames associated with them.

Security professionals can use tools and scripts to analyze DNS logs and records, looking for unusual or irregular domain name resolutions. Patterns such as subdomains, non-standard naming conventions, or uncommon DNS record types may indicate the presence of hidden services.

Passive DNS analysis can be complemented with active DNS enumeration techniques, such as DNS zone transfers, to gather comprehensive information about the network's DNS infrastructure and discover hidden services.

Additionally, exploring the use of unconventional or less-known protocols and communication channels can help detect hidden services. Hidden services may utilize protocols and channels that are not widely monitored or inspected, making them less visible to traditional security measures.

Security professionals can use network analysis tools to search for unusual or unexpected protocol activity. For example, unusual traffic patterns on less-known ports or the use of non-standard communication protocols can be indicative of hidden services.

Furthermore, employing open-source intelligence (OSINT) techniques can provide valuable information for detecting hidden services. OSINT involves collecting and analyzing publicly available information, such as domain registrations, WHOIS data, and online forums, to uncover hidden services and their associated infrastructure.

By conducting OSINT investigations, security professionals can gather clues about hidden services, including domain names, IP addresses, and potential affiliations with malicious actors.

In summary, detecting hidden services is a critical aspect of network security and penetration testing, as these services may pose security risks or vulnerabilities. Security professionals and ethical hackers employ various techniques and tools, including active scanning, network traffic analysis, passive DNS analysis, exploration of unconventional protocols, and open-source intelligence (OSINT) investigations, to uncover hidden services within a network.

Active scanning involves sending specific probes to known ports, while network traffic analysis examines packet payloads and communication patterns. Passive DNS analysis focuses on DNS resolution data, and exploration of unconventional protocols looks for unusual or non-standard protocol activity.

By utilizing a combination of these techniques, security professionals can gain insights into hidden services, assess their potential impact on network security, and take appropriate measures to mitigate risks.

Chapter 5: Vulnerability Scanning with NMAP

Automating vulnerability checks is a fundamental practice in the field of cybersecurity and network defense. Vulnerabilities in software, applications, and systems can expose organizations to various security risks, and regularly checking for and addressing these vulnerabilities is crucial to maintaining a secure network environment.

Vulnerability checks involve the process of identifying and assessing weaknesses or flaws in software, configurations, or hardware components that could be exploited by attackers. These checks can encompass a wide range of potential vulnerabilities, including software vulnerabilities, misconfigurations, outdated software, and more.

Automation plays a significant role in streamlining and enhancing the efficiency of vulnerability checks. Automated tools and scripts can help security professionals and system administrators quickly and comprehensively scan networks and systems for vulnerabilities.

One of the widely used tools for automating vulnerability checks is Nessus. Nessus is a popular vulnerability scanning tool that enables organizations to perform automated scans of their networks, servers, and applications to identify potential vulnerabilities.

To initiate a vulnerability scan using Nessus, security professionals can use the following command:

```
nessuscmd -q -T html -R [Report Name] -i [Scan Policy]
-x [Scan Export] -c [Hosts] -p [Port Range]
```

Replace "[Report Name]" with the desired name for the scan report, "[Scan Policy]" with the selected scan policy, "[Scan Export]" with the export file format (e.g., html), "[Hosts]" with the target hosts or IP addresses, and "[Port Range]" with the range of ports to be scanned.

Nessus scans are highly configurable, allowing users to tailor scans to their specific needs. Users can define scan policies, select scan options, and customize the scope of the scan based on their requirements.

Another widely used tool for automated vulnerability checks is OpenVAS (Open Vulnerability Assessment System). OpenVAS is an open-source vulnerability scanner that provides a comprehensive database of known vulnerabilities and a user-friendly interface for conducting scans.

To initiate a vulnerability scan using OpenVAS, security professionals can use the following command:

openvas-cli --target [Target] --config [Config File] --report [Report Name] --vulnerability [Vulnerability ID]

Replace "[Target]" with the target host or IP address, "[Config File]" with the desired configuration file, "[Report Name]" with the name of the scan report, and "[Vulnerability ID]" with the specific vulnerability to be checked.

OpenVAS offers predefined scan configurations and vulnerability checks, making it easier for users to conduct scans and identify potential vulnerabilities.

Automated vulnerability checks can also be performed using command-line scripts and custom tools. For example, security professionals can write scripts in languages like Python or Bash to automate vulnerability checks and integrate them into their existing workflows.

These custom scripts can leverage vulnerability databases, APIs, or network scanning libraries to identify and assess vulnerabilities on target systems.

Automation scripts can also be used to schedule regular vulnerability scans, ensuring that systems are continuously monitored for new vulnerabilities and security risks.

In addition to Nessus and OpenVAS, there are other commercial and open-source vulnerability scanning tools available that offer automation capabilities. These tools vary in features, scalability, and supported platforms, allowing organizations to choose the most suitable solution based on their specific needs and budget.

Automated vulnerability checks are not limited to scanning for known vulnerabilities. They can also encompass checks for misconfigurations, compliance with security policies, and adherence to best practices.

For example, organizations can use automated tools to scan their systems and configurations for compliance with industry standards such as CIS (Center for Internet Security) benchmarks or specific security policies and guidelines.

Automated vulnerability checks help organizations prioritize and remediate vulnerabilities based on their severity and potential impact. Vulnerability scanning tools typically provide vulnerability assessments with risk scores or severity ratings, allowing organizations to focus their efforts on addressing the most critical vulnerabilities first.

Automation also facilitates the tracking and management of vulnerabilities. Vulnerability management platforms can automate the process of tracking, prioritizing, and assigning vulnerabilities to relevant teams or individuals for remediation.

These platforms can integrate with ticketing systems, provide dashboards for real-time vulnerability status updates, and generate reports to demonstrate compliance with security policies and regulations.

To maintain the effectiveness of automated vulnerability checks, organizations should keep their vulnerability databases and scanning tools up to date. Vulnerability databases are continuously updated with new vulnerabilities, patches, and security advisories, so regularly updating the scanning tools ensures that they have the latest information for accurate assessments.

It's essential to consider the potential impact of automated vulnerability checks on the target systems. Scanning tools can generate network traffic and generate logs on the target, which may be detected by network intrusion detection systems (IDS) or generate false positives in some cases.

To mitigate these concerns, security professionals can use techniques such as stealth scanning or slow scanning, which adjust the scanning speed and timing to minimize the impact on target systems and network defenses.

In summary, automating vulnerability checks is a critical practice for maintaining network security and mitigating potential risks. Vulnerabilities in software, configurations, and systems can be exploited by attackers, making regular vulnerability assessments essential.

Tools like Nessus, OpenVAS, and custom scripts enable security professionals and system administrators to automate vulnerability checks and identify potential weaknesses efficiently.

Automated vulnerability checks extend beyond scanning for known vulnerabilities and can include checks for misconfigurations, compliance with security policies, and adherence to industry standards.

Organizations should keep their scanning tools and vulnerability databases up to date to ensure accurate assessments and prioritize remediation efforts based on severity.

Overall, automation streamlines the vulnerability management process and enhances an organization's ability to maintain a secure network environment.

Integrating NMAP with vulnerability databases is a powerful approach that enhances the effectiveness of network reconnaissance and security assessment. Vulnerability databases contain comprehensive information about known vulnerabilities in various software, applications, and systems, making them invaluable resources for security professionals.

By integrating NMAP, a versatile network scanning tool, with vulnerability databases, security professionals can perform more informed and targeted scans, identify potential security risks, and prioritize remediation efforts effectively.

One of the primary ways to integrate NMAP with vulnerability databases is by using NSE (NMAP Scripting Engine) scripts. NSE scripts are custom scripts written in Lua that extend the functionality of NMAP.

Several NSE scripts are designed to retrieve vulnerability information from various databases and incorporate it into NMAP scans.

For example, the "vulners" NSE script allows security professionals to search for known vulnerabilities in NMAP scans using the Vulners.com vulnerability database. To use this script, the following NMAP command can be executed:

nmap -p 80 --script vulners.nse [Target]

Replace "[Target]" with the target system's IP address or hostname.

The "vulners" script will scan the specified target and search the Vulners.com database for known vulnerabilities related to the scanned services.

Similarly, the "cve-search" NSE script can be employed to query the CVE (Common Vulnerabilities and Exposures) database for known vulnerabilities.

To use the "cve-search" script, security professionals can execute the following NMAP command:

nmap --script cve-search --script-args searchstring=[Search Term] [Target]

Replace "[Search Term]" with the specific term you want to search for in the CVE database, and "[Target]" with the target system's IP address or hostname.

Integrating NMAP with vulnerability databases provides several advantages. First, it enables security professionals to identify potential vulnerabilities during the initial network reconnaissance phase, allowing for more targeted and efficient scans.

Second, it allows for the prioritization of vulnerabilities based on their severity and potential impact. By retrieving information from vulnerability databases, security professionals can assign risk scores or severity ratings to identified vulnerabilities and address the most critical ones first.

Third, NMAP's integration with vulnerability databases enhances reporting capabilities. Scans can include detailed information about identified vulnerabilities, making it easier to communicate findings to stakeholders and demonstrate the need for remediation.

Additionally, security professionals can integrate NMAP with various vulnerability assessment platforms and security information and event management (SIEM) systems.

These integrations enable automated vulnerability scanning, continuous monitoring, and real-time threat detection.

For example, NMAP scans and results can be integrated with platforms like Tenable Nessus or Rapid7 Nexpose to provide comprehensive vulnerability assessment and management.

Integrating NMAP with SIEM systems allows organizations to correlate network scan data with other security events and logs, providing a holistic view of network security.

When integrating NMAP with vulnerability databases, it's essential to consider the accuracy and completeness of the databases. Vulnerability databases may not always have the latest information or cover every possible vulnerability.

Therefore, security professionals should use multiple databases and cross-reference their findings to ensure comprehensive coverage.

Furthermore, NMAP's integration with vulnerability databases should be done with proper authorization and in compliance with ethical guidelines. Scanning systems and networks without proper authorization can lead to legal and ethical issues.

Organizations should obtain consent from network owners and stakeholders before conducting vulnerability scans and should follow responsible disclosure practices when identifying and reporting vulnerabilities.

In summary, integrating NMAP with vulnerability databases is a valuable practice for security professionals and organizations seeking to enhance their network reconnaissance and security assessment capabilities.

By leveraging NSE scripts and querying databases like Vulners.com or CVE, security professionals can identify potential vulnerabilities, prioritize remediation efforts, and improve reporting capabilities.

Integrations with vulnerability assessment platforms and SIEM systems further streamline the vulnerability management process and enable automated scanning and continuous monitoring.

However, it's essential to ensure the accuracy and completeness of the databases used and conduct scans responsibly and ethically with proper authorization.

Chapter 6: Network Mapping and Topology Discovery

Creating detailed network maps is a crucial step in understanding and managing complex network environments. Network maps provide a visual representation of the network's structure, including devices, connections, and configurations, which can be invaluable for troubleshooting, security assessments, and network optimization.

Network maps come in various forms, ranging from simple diagrams to sophisticated interactive models, and their complexity often depends on the size and complexity of the network being mapped.

One of the first considerations when creating network maps is selecting the appropriate tools and techniques. There are numerous tools available for creating network maps, ranging from open-source software to commercial solutions.

One widely used open-source tool for creating network maps is NMAP. NMAP, primarily known as a network scanning tool, also offers network mapping capabilities that can generate simple network diagrams by discovering and mapping devices and their relationships.

To create a basic network map using NMAP, you can use the following command:

nmap -sn -oX [Output File] [Target Network]

Replace "[Output File]" with the desired filename for the XML output and "[Target Network]" with the network range or IP address of the target network.

The "-sn" option instructs NMAP to perform a ping scan to discover live hosts, while the "-oX" option specifies the output format as XML.

Once the scan is completed, you can use a tool like Zenmap, a graphical user interface (GUI) for NMAP, to convert the XML output into a more visually appealing network map.

While NMAP can generate basic network maps, it may not provide the level of detail and customization required for complex networks.

For larger and more intricate networks, dedicated network mapping tools like SolarWinds Network Topology Mapper, NetBrain, or Microsoft Visio, can be more suitable.

These tools often offer features such as auto-discovery of devices, customizable templates, and advanced mapping options to create detailed and tailored network maps.

When creating detailed network maps, it's essential to start with a clear understanding of the network's goals and objectives. Consider what information you want to convey with the map and who the intended audience is.

For example, a network map for a small business may focus on device locations and connections, while a network map for an enterprise may include additional details like VLANs, subnets, and traffic flows.

The mapping process typically begins with device discovery, which involves identifying all the devices connected to the network. This can be done using a combination of network scanning tools, SNMP (Simple Network Management Protocol), and manual inspection.

Once devices are discovered, their relationships and connections should be documented. This includes identifying routers, switches, access points, servers, workstations, and any other networked devices.

Network topology plays a significant role in creating accurate network maps. Understanding how devices are interconnected, including the physical and logical connections, helps ensure the map reflects the network's true structure.

For example, mapping VLANs and subnets can provide insights into network segmentation and routing. It's also essential to document the IP addressing scheme, naming conventions, and any special configurations or policies in place.

To represent the network visually, consider using symbols and labels that are intuitive and easily understood by the intended audience. Using color coding for different device types or status indicators (e.g., up/down) can make the map more informative.

As the network map evolves, it's crucial to keep it up to date. Networks are dynamic, with devices being added, removed, or reconfigured regularly.

Automated network mapping tools can help maintain accuracy by periodically scanning the network and updating the map automatically.

Creating detailed network maps also serves security and troubleshooting purposes. In the event of network issues or security incidents, having an up-to-date map can expedite the identification of affected devices and their relationships.

Furthermore, network maps can be used for capacity planning, performance monitoring, and compliance assessments. They provide a holistic view of the network, helping organizations make informed decisions and ensure compliance with security policies and regulations.

In summary, creating detailed network maps is a fundamental practice for understanding, managing, and optimizing network environments. Whether using tools like NMAP for simple maps or dedicated network mapping solutions for complex networks, accurate and up-to-date maps provide valuable insights into device relationships, configurations, and network topology.

Consider the network's goals and audience, and use clear symbols and labels to represent devices and connections effectively.

Regularly update the map to reflect network changes and use it for troubleshooting, security assessments, and compliance monitoring.

A well-maintained network map is an indispensable tool for network administrators and security professionals alike.

Discovering complex network topologies is a critical task for understanding and managing intricate and interconnected network environments. Complex network topologies can involve a wide range of devices, connections, and configurations, and gaining visibility into these structures is essential for ensuring efficient network operations, troubleshooting issues, and enhancing security.

To embark on the journey of discovering complex network topologies, it's important to employ the right tools and techniques. One valuable tool for network discovery is NMAP, a versatile network scanning and mapping tool.

Using NMAP, network administrators and security professionals can initiate scans to discover and map the devices and services within a network. One commonly used NMAP scan for network discovery is the ping scan, which can help identify live hosts.

To perform a ping scan with NMAP, you can use the following command:

nmap -sn [Target Network]

Replace "[Target Network]" with the IP address range or network you want to scan.

The "-sn" option instructs NMAP to perform a simple ping scan, which sends ICMP Echo Requests to potential hosts to determine if they are online.

While a basic ping scan can identify live hosts, discovering complex network topologies often requires more in-depth scanning and mapping techniques.

One such technique is the use of the "-A" option with NMAP, which enables the OS detection and version detection features. This can provide valuable information about the operating systems and services running on discovered devices.

For example, you can initiate a more comprehensive scan with NMAP like this:

nmap - A [Target]

Replace "[Target]" with the specific target host or network you want to scan.

The "-A" option instructs NMAP to enable advanced scanning and detection features, which can help identify the types of devices and services present in the network.

To discover complex network topologies, it's essential to consider the different types of devices and their roles within the network. Devices can include routers, switches, firewalls, servers, workstations, and various networked appliances.

By understanding the roles and responsibilities of these devices, network administrators can gain insights into the network's structure and hierarchy.

Network documentation is a valuable resource for discovering complex network topologies. It includes information about device configurations, network segments, IP address assignments, VLANs (Virtual Local Area Networks), subnets, and routing tables.

Examining documentation can reveal how devices are interconnected and what routing and switching protocols are in use.

Network monitoring tools also play a significant role in discovering complex network topologies. Tools like

Wireshark, Nagios, or PRTG Network Monitor can capture and analyze network traffic, providing insights into device communication patterns and network flows.

These tools can help identify bottlenecks, performance issues, and potential security threats within the network.

Additionally, network administrators can leverage SNMP (Simple Network Management Protocol) to gather information about network devices. SNMP enables the querying of device configurations, status, and performance metrics.

To use SNMP to discover network topologies, administrators need to configure SNMP on network devices and use SNMP management software to query and collect data.

Understanding routing and switching protocols is crucial for discovering complex network topologies. Protocols like OSPF (Open Shortest Path First), BGP (Border Gateway Protocol), and spanning tree protocols play a significant role in determining how data flows within the network and how devices are interconnected.

By examining the routing tables and topology databases maintained by these protocols, network administrators can gain insights into the network's structure.

Network discovery tools, such as the open-source tool "netdisco," can automate the process of discovering complex network topologies. Netdisco uses SNMP and other protocols to collect data about devices, VLANs, IP addresses, and port-to-MAC address mappings.

Once the data is collected, Netdisco generates network maps and visualizations that provide a clear view of device interconnections and network segments.

Visualizations, such as network diagrams or tree diagrams, can aid in understanding complex network topologies by representing devices, links, and their relationships graphically.

Regularly updating and maintaining network documentation and using network discovery tools can help keep network topologies accurate and up to date.

In summary, discovering complex network topologies is a fundamental task for network administrators and security professionals. Tools like NMAP, network documentation, network monitoring tools, SNMP, and network discovery tools are invaluable for gaining visibility into intricate network structures.

Understanding device roles, routing and switching protocols, and data flows within the network is essential for comprehending the network's hierarchy and interconnections.

Regular updates and maintenance of network documentation and the use of network discovery tools are crucial for keeping network topologies accurate and reflective of the ever-evolving network environment.

A thorough understanding of complex network topologies enables organizations to optimize network performance, troubleshoot issues effectively, and enhance network security.

Chapter 7: Evading IDS/IPS with NMAP

In the realm of network security, intrusion detection systems (IDS) and intrusion prevention systems (IPS) play pivotal roles in safeguarding networks and systems against potential threats. These systems are designed to monitor network traffic and detect suspicious or malicious activities, providing an essential layer of defense in a comprehensive security strategy.

However, as with any security measure, there are those who seek to bypass or evade IDS/IPS systems in their pursuit of unauthorized access or attacks. IDS/IPS evasion techniques encompass a range of strategies and tactics employed by malicious actors to circumvent detection or mitigation by these security systems.

One of the fundamental techniques used to evade IDS/IPS is known as fragmentation. Fragmentation involves breaking up network packets into smaller fragments, which can make it more challenging for these systems to detect malicious payloads or patterns.

To fragment packets, attackers can use tools like "hping3" or "scapy" with specific command-line options.

For instance, with "hping3," an attacker can issue a command like:

hping3 --flood -d 120 -S -w 64 -p 80 --fragment -a 192.168.1.1 [Target]

In this command, the "--fragment" option instructs "hping3" to send fragmented packets, potentially evading IDS/IPS detection.

Another common evasion technique involves encoding or obfuscating malicious payloads. Attackers may use techniques like URL encoding, base64 encoding, or custom encoding schemes to hide the true nature of their payloads.

For example, a payload that triggers an IDS/IPS rule might be encoded as follows:

perl

%3C%73%63%72%69%70%74%3E%61%6C%65%72%74

%28%27%48%61%63%6B%65%64%27%29%3B%3C%2F

%73%63%72%69%70%74%3E

By encoding the payload, attackers aim to evade signature-based detection mechanisms used by IDS/IPS.

Another evasion technique involves the manipulation of packet header fields. By altering the header information, attackers can deceive IDS/IPS systems into misinterpreting or ignoring network traffic.

For instance, attackers might manipulate the IP time-to-live (TTL) field, TCP flags, or packet sequencing to make traffic appear legitimate or less suspicious.

Tools like "Scapy" can be used to craft and send packets with modified header fields.

DNS tunneling is another evasion technique where attackers use DNS (Domain Name System) traffic to transmit malicious data or establish covert communication channels. By encapsulating data within DNS requests or responses, attackers can evade detection by blending malicious traffic with legitimate DNS traffic.

To deploy DNS tunneling, attackers may use tools like "Iodine" or custom scripts to encode and decode data within DNS packets.

Intrusion detection systems often rely on known signatures or patterns to detect malicious activities. To evade these signature-based detections, attackers may employ polymorphic malware, which constantly changes its appearance or behavior.

Polymorphic malware can generate new variants with each execution, making it challenging for IDS/IPS systems to keep up with the evolving threat.

Another evasion technique is to exploit protocol vulnerabilities. Attackers may manipulate protocol behaviors or take advantage of ambiguities in protocol implementations to bypass IDS/IPS systems.

For example, some IDS/IPS systems may not effectively handle IPv6 traffic or may have weaknesses in their handling of specific protocols like FTP (File Transfer Protocol) or SMB (Server Message Block).

Evasion through protocol exploitation often requires in-depth knowledge of protocol specifications and implementations.

Another evasion strategy is to launch low-and-slow attacks. Rather than bombarding a target with a high volume of traffic, attackers send small, slow, and sporadic packets to avoid triggering IDS/IPS alarms.

By operating below the detection threshold of these systems, attackers can quietly conduct reconnaissance or establish a foothold within a network.

Advanced evasion techniques involve the use of polymorphic shellcodes. Polymorphic shellcodes mutate with each use, making it challenging for IDS/IPS systems to identify and block them.

Attackers may employ polymorphic engines or generation tools to create these ever-changing shellcodes, exploiting vulnerabilities or executing malicious payloads without detection.

Some attackers leverage encrypted communication channels to hide malicious activities from IDS/IPS systems. By encrypting network traffic using secure protocols like HTTPS or encrypted tunnels like VPNs (Virtual Private Networks), attackers can mask the content of their communication.

To further obfuscate their actions, attackers may use encryption with steganography, hiding data within images or other innocuous files.

IDS/IPS evasion techniques continue to evolve, necessitating ongoing efforts by security professionals to stay ahead of attackers. To mitigate the risk of evasion, organizations should implement multi-layered security strategies that include anomaly detection, behavioral analysis, and threat intelligence in addition to signature-based detection.

Regularly updating and fine-tuning IDS/IPS rule sets is crucial to adapt to emerging evasion tactics and maintain network security.

By understanding these evasion techniques and proactively defending against them, organizations can bolster their network defenses and minimize the risk of falling victim to sophisticated attacks.

Stealth scanning methods are a critical component of NMAP's arsenal, allowing network administrators and security professionals to perform reconnaissance and vulnerability assessment without arousing suspicion or triggering intrusion detection systems (IDS). These stealthy techniques enable users to gather valuable information about target systems and networks discreetly, which can be invaluable for security assessments and penetration testing.

One of the most commonly used stealth scanning methods in NMAP is the TCP SYN scan, also known as half-open scanning. This technique involves sending a TCP SYN packet to the target's ports to determine if they are open, closed, or filtered.

To execute a TCP SYN scan with NMAP, you can use the following command:

nmap -sS [Target]

Replace "[Target]" with the specific target's IP address or hostname.

The "-sS" option instructs NMAP to perform a TCP SYN scan.

The advantage of the TCP SYN scan is that it does not complete the full TCP handshake, making it less likely to trigger IDS alerts compared to full-connect scans. However, it can still provide valuable information about open ports and services on the target system.

Another stealth scanning method used in NMAP is the TCP FIN scan. In this technique, NMAP sends a TCP FIN packet to the target's ports and analyzes the responses to determine their state.

To execute a TCP FIN scan with NMAP, you can use the following command:

nmap -sF [Target]

Replace "[Target]" with the target's IP address or hostname.

The "-sF" option instructs NMAP to perform a TCP FIN scan.

TCP FIN scans work by sending a TCP FIN (finish) flag to the target's ports. If a port is open, it should respond with a TCP RST (reset) packet, indicating that the port is closed. If a port is closed, it may either ignore the packet or respond with a TCP RST packet. Filtered ports, on the other hand, may not respond at all, making them more challenging to differentiate from closed ports.

One of the stealthiest scanning methods in NMAP is the TCP NULL scan. In this technique, NMAP sends TCP packets with no flags set (NULL packets) to the target's ports and analyzes the responses.

To execute a TCP NULL scan with NMAP, you can use the following command:

nmap -sN [Target]

Replace "[Target]" with the target's IP address or hostname.

The "-sN" option instructs NMAP to perform a TCP NULL scan.

TCP NULL scans rely on the behavior of target systems and their interpretation of RFC (Request for Comments) specifications. The idea is that if a port is open, it should not respond to a NULL packet, while a closed port should respond with a TCP RST packet.

Another stealth scanning technique is the TCP Xmas scan. Similar to the TCP NULL scan, the Xmas scan sends packets with various TCP flags set to create an unusual combination of flags.

To execute a TCP Xmas scan with NMAP, you can use the following command:

nmap -sX [Target]

Replace "[Target]" with the target's IP address or hostname.

The "-sX" option instructs NMAP to perform a TCP Xmas scan.

TCP Xmas scans set the URG, PSH, and FIN flags in the TCP packet header. The scan relies on the behavior of target systems, with open ports typically not responding, while closed ports respond with a TCP RST packet.

One more stealth scanning method is the TCP ACK scan, which involves sending TCP ACK (acknowledgment) packets to the target's ports. The purpose of this scan is to determine whether a firewall is present and whether it permits access to specific ports.

To execute a TCP ACK scan with NMAP, you can use the following command:

nmap -sA [Target]

Replace "[Target]" with the target's IP address or hostname.

The "-sA" option instructs NMAP to perform a TCP ACK scan.

In a TCP ACK scan, open ports typically do not respond, while closed ports respond with a TCP RST packet. Firewalls, on the other hand, may respond differently, indicating whether they allow or block access to specific ports.

It's important to note that while stealth scanning methods can help avoid triggering IDS alerts, they may not always provide complete or accurate information about target systems. Firewalls, intrusion prevention systems, and network configurations can influence how ports respond to these scans.

Additionally, the effectiveness of stealth scanning methods may vary depending on the target's operating system and configuration.

Security professionals and ethical hackers should use stealth scans responsibly and within the scope of authorized assessments to avoid legal and ethical issues.

In summary, NMAP offers a range of stealth scanning methods that enable network administrators and security professionals to discreetly gather information about target systems and networks. These techniques, including TCP SYN scans, TCP FIN scans, TCP NULL scans, TCP Xmas scans, and TCP ACK scans, allow users to assess open ports, identify potential vulnerabilities, and evaluate firewall behavior.

While stealth scans can help evade detection, they may not always provide a complete picture of a target's security posture. Security practitioners should use these techniques responsibly and with proper authorization to ensure the safety and legality of their assessments.

Chapter 8: Data Analysis and Visualization

Analyzing NMAP output data is a crucial skill for network administrators and security professionals, as it provides valuable insights into the state and security of a network. NMAP, as a versatile network scanning tool, generates a wealth of information about the devices, services, and vulnerabilities present on a target network.

When conducting network scans with NMAP, it's important to understand the various output formats that the tool can produce. NMAP offers several output options, including plain text, XML, and grepable formats, each suited to different analysis needs.

To specify the output format of an NMAP scan, you can use the "-o" option followed by the desired format. For example, to generate XML output, you can use the following command:

nmap -oX scan_output.xml [Target]

Replace "[Target]" with the target's IP address or hostname.

The "-oX" option instructs NMAP to save the scan results in XML format.

XML output is highly structured and can be easily parsed and processed by automated tools, making it a preferred choice for in-depth analysis and integration with other security software.

Once you have conducted an NMAP scan and obtained the output data, the next step is to interpret and analyze the results. Start by opening the output file in a text editor or

XML viewer to get a sense of the data's structure and content.

One of the essential pieces of information provided by NMAP is the list of open ports on the target system. This information is valuable for understanding the attack surface of the network and identifying potential entry points for malicious actors.

In the NMAP output, open ports are typically listed along with their associated service names and version information. By examining this data, you can determine which services are running on the target and assess whether any of them have known vulnerabilities.

For example, if NMAP reports that port 22 is open and the service is identified as "SSH," you can research the current state of SSH security and any recent vulnerabilities that may affect it.

NMAP also provides information about the state of the target system's operating system. This is done through a process called OS fingerprinting, where NMAP attempts to identify the OS based on various network behaviors and responses.

In the NMAP output, you can find details about the OS fingerprinting results, including the most likely operating system and a confidence level. Keep in mind that OS fingerprinting is not always 100% accurate, but it can provide valuable insights into the target environment.

In addition to open ports and OS information, NMAP generates data related to service versions. This includes details about the software versions running on the open ports.

Analyzing service version data is crucial for assessing the potential vulnerabilities associated with specific services.

By knowing the software versions, you can cross-reference them with vulnerability databases to determine if any known security issues exist.

For example, if NMAP reports that the HTTP service running on port 80 is Apache version 2.4.41, you can search for vulnerabilities associated with that specific version to gauge the potential risk.

NMAP also includes valuable information about the existence of NMAP scripts or NSE (NMAP Scripting Engine) scripts. These scripts are custom-made or community-contributed scripts that can perform various tasks, such as service enumeration, vulnerability scanning, or information gathering.

In the NMAP output, you can find details about which NSE scripts were executed during the scan and what results they produced. This information can be particularly useful for automating repetitive tasks and conducting specialized assessments.

Interpreting NMAP output often involves searching for patterns or anomalies in the data. Look for unexpected or unusual findings, such as open ports that shouldn't be open, outdated service versions, or unexpected software running on certain ports.

For example, if NMAP reveals that an FTP service is running on a non-standard port like 8080, it may warrant further investigation to determine if it's a legitimate configuration or a potential security concern.

To aid in the analysis of NMAP output, consider using tools like NSE scripts or third-party vulnerability scanners that can complement NMAP's findings. These tools can help automate the process of identifying vulnerabilities and assessing the overall security posture of the target network.

Moreover, NMAP allows users to save scan results in various output formats, making it possible to generate reports tailored to specific needs. For instance, you can convert NMAP's XML output into more user-friendly formats like HTML or PDF using tools like "xsltproc" or dedicated reporting software.

In summary, analyzing NMAP output data is a critical step in assessing the security and state of a network. NMAP provides valuable information about open ports, operating systems, service versions, and the presence of custom scripts.

By carefully reviewing and interpreting this data, network administrators and security professionals can identify potential vulnerabilities, assess the network's security posture, and take proactive steps to mitigate risks.

Understanding the capabilities of NMAP and its various output formats allows for more effective analysis and informed decision-making when it comes to network security.

Visualizing network scanning results is a powerful way to gain deeper insights into the security and structure of a network. While raw data from tools like NMAP provides valuable information, visual representations can make complex findings more accessible and understandable.

One of the most common and effective ways to visualize network scanning results is through network topology diagrams. These diagrams illustrate the layout of a network, including devices, connections, and open ports, helping security professionals and network administrators understand the network's structure.

To create network topology diagrams, you can use various tools and techniques. One popular option is to use dedicated network mapping tools like "NMAP Topology" or "NetBrain." These tools can automatically generate visual representations of a network based on the data gathered during a scanning process.

For example, you can use the following NMAP command to scan a network and generate XML output:

nmap -oX scan_output.xml [Target]

Then, you can import the XML output into a network mapping tool to create a visual diagram of the network.

Network topology diagrams typically display devices as nodes and connections as lines or arrows between them. Open ports and services associated with each device can be labeled within the nodes, providing a comprehensive view of the network's components.

Another visualization technique involves heatmaps, which are graphical representations that use color-coding to convey information. In the context of network scanning results, heatmaps can be used to visualize the severity of vulnerabilities or the concentration of open ports across the network.

To create vulnerability heatmaps, you can use spreadsheet software or specialized vulnerability management tools. First, export the relevant data from your network scanning tool, including information about vulnerabilities and their severity levels.

For example, NMAP can be configured to output XML data containing vulnerability information. Once you have this data, you can import it into a spreadsheet application and use conditional formatting to apply color-coding based on the severity of each vulnerability.

In the heatmap, vulnerabilities with higher severity levels can be represented in red or orange, while lower-severity vulnerabilities may appear in yellow or green. This visual representation allows you to quickly identify critical areas of concern within the network.

Additionally, heatmaps can be used to visualize the distribution of open ports across devices. For example, you can create a heatmap to show which devices have the highest number of open ports, helping you identify potential security risks or misconfigurations.

Visualization techniques can also extend to the display of network traffic patterns. Tools like "Wireshark" can capture and analyze network traffic, providing valuable insights into the communication between devices.

To visualize network traffic patterns, you can use the built-in features of Wireshark or export data to other visualization tools. Wireshark offers options to display traffic as flow diagrams, pie charts, or time-series graphs.

Flow diagrams illustrate the connections and communication between devices, making it easier to identify unusual or suspicious traffic patterns. Pie charts can show the distribution of traffic by protocol or source/destination, helping you understand the network's usage.

Time-series graphs provide insights into network activity trends over time, which can be valuable for detecting anomalies or identifying periods of high traffic.

Another effective way to visualize network scanning results is through the use of geographic maps. Geographic maps can help you understand the physical distribution of devices and their associated open ports.

To create geographic maps, you can use geospatial visualization tools like "Google Maps" or "OpenStreetMap." First, collect information about the geographical location of each device in your network.

This can be done manually by recording the physical location of devices or by using tools that can determine the geographical coordinates of devices based on IP addresses.

Once you have the geographical data, you can plot devices on the map and overlay open ports or vulnerabilities using color-coded markers. This visual representation provides a geographic perspective on your network's security posture and distribution.

Visualization techniques are not limited to post-scan analysis; they can also be applied in real-time for monitoring and intrusion detection. Tools like "Elasticsearch" and "Kibana" can ingest NMAP scan results and create real-time dashboards with visualizations that display network activity.

For example, you can configure Elasticsearch to index NMAP scan data and set up Kibana to create visualizations such as bar charts, line graphs, or pie charts based on the data. These visualizations can help security teams monitor network activity and detect anomalies or unauthorized access in real-time.

In summary, visualizing network scanning results enhances the understanding and interpretation of complex data. Network topology diagrams, vulnerability heatmaps, traffic patterns, geographic maps, and real-time dashboards all offer valuable perspectives on a network's security and structure.

By employing appropriate visualization techniques and tools, security professionals and network administrators can make informed decisions, prioritize remediation efforts, and enhance the overall security posture of their networks.

Visual representations of network scanning results provide a means to communicate findings effectively within organizations, helping stakeholders grasp the significance of security issues and take appropriate actions to mitigate risks.

Chapter 9: NMAP in Penetration Testing

Using NMAP for initial reconnaissance is a fundamental step in understanding a target network's structure and identifying potential vulnerabilities. Reconnaissance is often the first phase of a security assessment, whether it's a penetration test, vulnerability assessment, or network audit.

NMAP, as a versatile and powerful network scanning tool, plays a crucial role in this phase by providing insights into the target's exposed services, open ports, and potential weaknesses. To effectively use NMAP for initial reconnaissance, it's essential to follow a structured approach and understand the various scanning techniques and options available.

The initial step in using NMAP for reconnaissance is to identify the target network or IP addresses you want to assess. This could be a single host, a range of IP addresses, or even an entire subnet.

To specify the target in NMAP, you can use the following command:

nmap [Target]

Replace "[Target]" with the IP address, hostname, or IP range you want to scan.

For example, if you want to scan a single host with the IP address 192.168.1.100, your NMAP command would look like this:

nmap 192.168.1.100

Once you've defined your target, the next step is to choose the appropriate scanning technique. NMAP offers several scan types, each serving a specific purpose.

One of the most common scan types for initial reconnaissance is the TCP SYN scan, also known as the half-open scan. This scan sends a TCP SYN packet to the target's ports to determine their state (open, closed, or filtered).

To perform a TCP SYN scan with NMAP, use the following command:

nmap -sS [Target]

The "-sS" option instructs NMAP to perform a TCP SYN scan.

Another useful scan type for reconnaissance is the UDP scan, which explores open UDP ports on the target. UDP ports are commonly used for services like DNS and DHCP, and scanning them can reveal potential vulnerabilities.

To execute a UDP scan with NMAP, you can use the following command:

nmap -sU [Target]

The "-sU" option tells NMAP to perform a UDP scan.

Additionally, NMAP provides the option to perform a comprehensive scan using the "-sC" option, which activates the NMAP Scripting Engine (NSE). NSE allows you to use predefined scripts to perform various tasks, including service enumeration and vulnerability detection.

To run NSE scripts during your scan, include the "-sC" option in your NMAP command:

nmap -sC [Target]

These are just a few examples of the scanning techniques you can use with NMAP. The choice of technique depends on your goals and the target environment, and it's often necessary to experiment with different scans to gather a complete picture.

As NMAP conducts the scan, it sends packets to the specified target(s) and receives responses. The results are then displayed, indicating the status of each scanned port and the associated service information.

Interpreting NMAP's output is a crucial part of initial reconnaissance. For each scanned port, NMAP provides information about its state (open, closed, or filtered), the service running on the port, and the version of the service.

An open port signifies that a service is listening and accessible. This information can be valuable for understanding the attack surface and identifying potential entry points.

A closed port indicates that no service is listening on the specified port. While this is generally considered more secure, it's essential to verify that ports are correctly closed to avoid potential security gaps.

A filtered port suggests that a firewall or other security device is actively blocking access to the port. Filtered ports can be informative about the network's security posture and its defensive measures.

In addition to port states, NMAP provides information about the detected services. This includes the service name, protocol (TCP or UDP), and version information if available.

For example, NMAP may identify port 80 as open and label it as the "HTTP" service with version information like "Apache/2.4.41." This data allows you to understand the types of services running on the target and assess their potential vulnerabilities.

As part of initial reconnaissance, it's essential to document and organize the scan results systematically. Creating a log or report that includes details about open ports, service information, and any anomalies or unexpected findings can be invaluable for later analysis and decision-making.

Furthermore, using NMAP's output in combination with other tools and techniques can enhance your reconnaissance efforts. For example, you can import NMAP scan results into vulnerability scanners or security information and event management (SIEM) systems for deeper analysis and correlation.

In summary, using NMAP for initial reconnaissance is a critical step in assessing the security of a target network. By following a structured approach, choosing appropriate scanning techniques, and interpreting the scan results effectively, security professionals can gain valuable insights into a network's structure, open ports, and potential vulnerabilities.

Initial reconnaissance with NMAP sets the stage for subsequent phases of security assessments, enabling organizations to prioritize security measures, address weaknesses, and enhance overall network security.

Leveraging NMAP for post-exploitation is a critical phase in penetration testing and ethical hacking, where the focus shifts from gaining initial access to maintaining access and extracting valuable information from a compromised system. After successfully penetrating a target, ethical hackers often need to maintain their presence on the compromised system, escalate privileges, and gather additional intelligence.

NMAP, although primarily known for its network scanning capabilities, offers features and scripts that can be useful during the post-exploitation phase. One of the primary objectives during post-exploitation is to enumerate the target system thoroughly, identify vulnerabilities, and gather sensitive data without raising suspicion or triggering alarms.

One common use of NMAP in post-exploitation is to conduct more targeted and discreet scans. Unlike the initial reconnaissance phase, where network scanning may be aggressive and comprehensive, post-exploitation scans should be subtle to avoid detection.

To execute a discreet scan with NMAP, you can use the following command:

nmap -sS -T2 -p 1-65535 -oA post_exploitation_scan [Target]

In this command, the "-sS" option specifies a TCP SYN scan, which is less likely to trigger intrusion detection systems (IDS) or firewalls. The "-T2" option sets the timing template to a slower, less aggressive mode, and the "-p 1-65535" option scans all 65,535 ports.

By using these options, you can perform a more cautious and stealthy scan while still obtaining valuable information about the target system's open ports and services.

Additionally, NMAP's scripting capabilities, particularly the NMAP Scripting Engine (NSE), can be leveraged for post-exploitation tasks. NSE scripts allow ethical hackers to automate various tasks, such as service enumeration, vulnerability scanning, and data gathering, without raising suspicion.

For instance, NMAP offers scripts for querying databases, extracting user lists, or identifying running processes. These scripts can be executed on the compromised system to gather critical information about user accounts, installed software, or network configurations.

To run an NSE script during post-exploitation, use the following command:

nmap -p [Port] --script [Script] [Target]

Replace "[Port]" with the specific port number you want to target, "[Script]" with the name of the NSE script, and

"[Target]" with the compromised system's IP address or hostname.

For example, to run an NSE script called "smb-enum-users" on port 445, which is commonly associated with Windows file sharing, you can use the following command:

nmap -p 445 --script smb-enum-users [Target]

Running such scripts can provide valuable information about user accounts and permissions on the compromised system, aiding in privilege escalation and data extraction.

Another valuable aspect of NMAP in post-exploitation is its ability to identify pivot points within a network. Once access to a single system is obtained, ethical hackers may want to explore and compromise other systems within the same network.

NMAP's scanning and scripting capabilities can assist in identifying potential pivot points, such as poorly configured or vulnerable devices. By scanning adjacent network segments and identifying open ports and services on neighboring systems, ethical hackers can determine which systems may be ripe for further exploitation.

To conduct a scan of adjacent network segments, you can use NMAP's "-sP" option to perform a ping scan to discover live hosts, followed by a more targeted scan using the "-p" option to enumerate open ports and services.

In addition to network scanning and scripting, NMAP can assist in the exfiltration of data from the compromised system. Ethical hackers may need to retrieve specific files or data from the target, and NMAP can be used to transfer this data securely.

NMAP includes a built-in tool called "Ncat," which is a versatile networking utility that can be used for data transfer, port forwarding, and more. To initiate a secure file transfer from the compromised system to an external server, you can use the following command:

ncat --ssl -l -p [ListeningPort] > [OutputFile]
Replace "[ListeningPort]" with the port number you want to use for the transfer and "[OutputFile]" with the name of the file you want to transfer.
On the external server, you can set up an Ncat listener to receive the data using a similar command:

ncat --ssl -l -p [ListeningPort] < [OutputFile]
This secure file transfer technique allows ethical hackers to exfiltrate data without raising suspicions on the compromised system.
It's crucial to emphasize that NMAP and its associated tools should only be used for ethical and legal purposes, such as security assessments, penetration testing, and network administration. Unauthorized or malicious use of NMAP or any hacking tools is illegal and unethical.
In summary, leveraging NMAP for post-exploitation is a valuable skill for ethical hackers and penetration testers. NMAP's discreet scanning options, scripting capabilities, network enumeration tools, and data exfiltration features provide essential tools for maintaining access, gathering intelligence, and moving laterally within a compromised network.
By using NMAP effectively during post-exploitation, ethical hackers can enhance their ability to assess a target's security, identify vulnerabilities, and extract valuable information while minimizing the risk of detection.

Chapter 10: Case Studies and Real-world Applications

NMAP is an incredibly versatile and powerful tool with a wide range of applications in practical scenarios, making it an indispensable asset for network administrators, security professionals, and system analysts. In real-world situations, NMAP can be employed to accomplish various tasks, from network troubleshooting to security assessments and beyond.

One of the most common practical scenarios for NMAP is network discovery and inventory. Network administrators often use NMAP to map out the devices on their network, helping them maintain an up-to-date inventory of all connected devices. This knowledge is essential for network management, asset tracking, and security monitoring.

To perform network discovery with NMAP, administrators can execute a simple ping scan using the following command:

nmap -sn [Target]

The "-sn" option instructs NMAP to perform a ping scan without actually probing open ports. This way, it quickly identifies active hosts on the network without causing any disruption.

Another practical use of NMAP is service discovery. Network administrators and security professionals rely on NMAP to identify which services are running on their networked devices. Understanding the services running on each device is crucial for both network management and security assessment.

To conduct service discovery with NMAP, you can use the following command:

nmap -sV [Target]

The "-sV" option tells NMAP to probe open ports and determine the version of the services running on those ports. This information is invaluable for identifying potential vulnerabilities and ensuring services are up to date.

In practical scenarios involving network security, NMAP plays a pivotal role in vulnerability assessment. Security professionals use NMAP to scan networks for open ports and services, subsequently identifying potential weaknesses or misconfigurations. By assessing the security posture of a network, organizations can take proactive measures to mitigate risks and secure their infrastructure.

To perform a vulnerability assessment with NMAP, you can use various scanning techniques. One common approach is to use the "-A" option, which enables OS detection, version detection, script scanning, and traceroute.

The command for such a comprehensive scan would look like this:

nmap -A [Target]

The "-A" option provides a wealth of information about the target system, including the operating system, version information, and potentially exploitable vulnerabilities. Security professionals can then prioritize remediation efforts based on the findings.

Another practical scenario involves firewall and access control list (ACL) analysis. NMAP can help administrators and security teams evaluate the effectiveness of their network defenses by testing which ports and services are accessible from both internal and external perspectives.

To analyze firewall rules and ACLs with NMAP, you can use the following command:

nmap -p [Ports] [Target]

Replace "[Ports]" with a comma-separated list of port numbers you want to test, and "[Target]" with the IP address or hostname of the device behind the firewall. This allows you to determine whether specific ports are open or closed, helping identify potential security gaps in the network's perimeter.

In practical scenarios involving network troubleshooting, NMAP is a valuable tool for diagnosing connectivity issues and pinpointing the root causes. Network administrators can use NMAP to check if specific ports are reachable or if certain services are available, helping them quickly identify network problems.

For example, to test whether a web server is responding on port 80, you can use the following NMAP command:

nmap -p 80 [Target]

If NMAP reports that port 80 is open, it indicates that the web server is accessible. However, if the scan shows that port 80 is closed or filtered, it suggests a connectivity issue that needs further investigation.

Moreover, NMAP is employed in practical scenarios related to network performance optimization. By scanning and analyzing network traffic patterns, administrators can identify bottlenecks, congestion points, and areas where network resources may be underutilized.

To assess network performance with NMAP, administrators can use the following command to capture and analyze network packets:

nmap --packet-trace [Target]

The "--packet-trace" option traces the packets exchanged during the scan, providing insights into network latency, packet loss, and potential performance issues. Analyzing this data helps optimize network configurations and improve overall performance.

In scenarios involving network audits and compliance, NMAP is a valuable tool for ensuring that network configurations align with industry standards and security policies. Organizations can use NMAP to scan their networked devices, checking for compliance with predefined security benchmarks and identifying deviations that may pose risks.

To conduct compliance checks with NMAP, administrators can utilize NSE scripts designed for this purpose. For example, the "smb-enum-shares" script can be used to check the sharing configuration of Windows devices, ensuring they comply with security policies.

The command to run this script would be:

```
nmap -p 139,445 --script smb-enum-shares [Target]
```

This command scans ports 139 and 445 (commonly associated with Windows file sharing) and uses the "smb-enum-shares" script to enumerate shared resources on the target, helping assess compliance.

In summary, NMAP is a versatile and indispensable tool in a wide range of practical scenarios. From network discovery and inventory to service discovery, vulnerability assessment, firewall analysis, network troubleshooting, performance optimization, and compliance checks, NMAP's capabilities make it an essential asset for network administrators, security professionals, and system analysts.

Understanding how to effectively deploy NMAP in these practical scenarios empowers organizations to manage and secure their networks more effectively, ensuring optimal performance and adherence to security standards.

Success stories and lessons learned from using NMAP in various real-world scenarios offer valuable insights into the tool's practical application and its impact on network management, security, and optimization.

One notable success story involves a global financial institution that faced the challenge of managing and securing its extensive network infrastructure. With thousands of devices distributed across multiple data centers, branch offices, and cloud environments, the organization needed a robust solution for network discovery and inventory management.

By implementing NMAP, the institution achieved remarkable success in creating an up-to-date inventory of all networked devices. They used NMAP's scanning capabilities to map their network, identify active hosts, and categorize devices based on their roles and functions. This comprehensive inventory significantly improved their network management efforts, enabling faster troubleshooting, more efficient asset tracking, and better resource allocation.

In another success story, a cybersecurity firm relied on NMAP during a red team engagement with a large e-commerce company. The objective was to assess the client's network defenses and identify vulnerabilities that could potentially be exploited by malicious actors.

The red team leveraged NMAP's scanning techniques to evaluate the external-facing network of the e-commerce company. By carefully crafting NMAP commands and timing options, they conducted discreet scans that accurately identified open ports, services, and potential attack vectors. This information allowed the red team to simulate real-world attack scenarios and provide the client with actionable recommendations for improving their security posture.

Additionally, NMAP's scripting capabilities played a crucial role in this success story. The red team used NSE scripts to automate tasks such as service enumeration, banner grabbing, and vulnerability scanning. These scripts helped uncover hidden weaknesses in the client's infrastructure, ultimately leading to more effective remediation efforts.

Lessons learned from these success stories underscore the importance of using NMAP strategically and responsibly. First and foremost, NMAP should be deployed with a clear purpose and scope, whether it's for network discovery, vulnerability assessment, or security testing. Having a well-defined objective ensures that NMAP's capabilities are utilized effectively and efficiently.

Moreover, understanding the limitations of NMAP is essential. While NMAP is a powerful tool, it may not provide a complete view of a network, especially in complex environments with advanced security measures. It's crucial to complement NMAP scans with other tools and techniques to obtain a comprehensive assessment of a network's security posture.

Additionally, practitioners should prioritize discretion when conducting scans, especially in security assessments. Aggressive scans can trigger intrusion detection systems and lead to unnecessary alarms or disruptions. Using NMAP's timing options, such as adjusting the scan speed with the "-T" option, helps strike the right balance between thoroughness and stealth.

Furthermore, NMAP's scripting capabilities, specifically the NSE, offer significant advantages in automating tasks and customizing scans. However, users should exercise caution and thoroughly test NSE scripts in controlled environments before deploying them in production. Incorrectly written or malicious scripts can lead to unintended consequences and potential security risks.

Another crucial lesson learned is the importance of documentation and reporting. Creating comprehensive logs and reports of NMAP scans is essential for tracking progress, documenting findings, and communicating results to stakeholders. These reports serve as valuable references for decision-makers and aid in the prioritization of security measures.

Finally, ethical and legal considerations are paramount when using NMAP. Users must ensure that they have the necessary permissions and authorization to conduct scans, especially in scenarios involving external networks or third-party systems. Respecting privacy and adhering to applicable laws and regulations is fundamental to ethical and responsible NMAP usage.

Success stories and lessons learned from the practical application of NMAP illustrate its significance in modern network management, security assessment, and optimization. By leveraging NMAP strategically, understanding its limitations, prioritizing discretion, harnessing scripting capabilities, documenting findings, and adhering to ethical and legal principles, organizations and security professionals can harness the full potential of this powerful tool while minimizing risks and maximizing benefits.

BOOK 3
NMAP SECURITY ESSENTIALS
PROTECTING NETWORKS WITH EXPERT SKILLS

ROB BOTWRIGHT

Chapter 1: Network Security Fundamentals

Understanding network security concepts is paramount in the digital age, where interconnectedness and data sharing are ubiquitous. Network security encompasses a wide range of principles, practices, and technologies that safeguard the confidentiality, integrity, and availability of information within a networked environment.

At its core, network security aims to protect sensitive data from unauthorized access, alterations, or disruptions. To comprehend network security fully, one must grasp fundamental concepts that underpin its principles and methodologies.

One foundational concept is the "security triad," consisting of three key elements: confidentiality, integrity, and availability. Confidentiality ensures that information is only accessible to authorized individuals or systems, preventing unauthorized disclosure. Integrity guarantees that data remains unaltered and trustworthy, safeguarding it against tampering or corruption. Availability ensures that data and services are consistently accessible to authorized users, preventing disruptions or downtime.

In network security, these three aspects are interrelated, and a breach in one area can affect the others. For example, a denial-of-service (DoS) attack can disrupt availability, potentially leading to a breach of confidentiality if sensitive data becomes exposed during the outage.

Another essential concept is the "attack surface," which represents the sum of all potential vulnerabilities within a network or system. Minimizing the attack surface is a fundamental principle in network security, as it reduces the number of potential entry points for attackers. Reducing the attack surface involves practices such as patching software, configuring firewalls, and implementing access controls.

Firewalls are a crucial component of network security, serving as a barrier between trusted internal networks and untrusted external networks, typically the internet. Firewalls use a set of rules to determine which network traffic is allowed or denied. This concept is vital for controlling inbound and outbound traffic, mitigating threats, and enforcing security policies.

Firewalls are configured using rules that specify how traffic should be handled. For instance, a common rule might allow incoming web traffic on port 80 to reach a web server while blocking all other incoming traffic. Understanding firewall rules and their implications is essential for effective network security.

Access control is another critical concept in network security, governing who can access specific resources and what actions they can perform. Access control can be implemented through user authentication, role-based access control (RBAC), and permissions. Properly configuring access control helps prevent unauthorized users from accessing sensitive data or systems.

Encryption is a cornerstone of network security, ensuring that data remains confidential even if intercepted. Encryption transforms plaintext data into ciphertext using encryption algorithms and keys. To decrypt the data, the recipient needs the appropriate decryption key. Implementing encryption for sensitive communications, such as online banking or secure messaging, is vital to maintaining confidentiality.

Intrusion detection and prevention systems (IDS/IPS) are network security tools that monitor network traffic for suspicious activities or patterns. An IDS identifies potential security threats, while an IPS takes action to block or mitigate those threats. These systems play a crucial role in early threat detection and response.

Virtual private networks (VPNs) are a network security technology that creates encrypted tunnels for secure communication over untrusted networks, such as the internet. VPNs provide confidentiality and integrity for data in transit, making them essential for remote work, data privacy, and secure communication.

Network segmentation is a strategy that involves dividing a network into smaller, isolated segments or subnetworks. Segmentation limits the lateral movement of attackers within a network and reduces the impact of a breach. Understanding network segmentation is vital for organizations seeking to enhance their network security posture.

Threat modeling is a systematic approach to identifying and mitigating potential threats to a network or system. It involves evaluating vulnerabilities, assessing the likelihood and impact of threats, and prioritizing security measures. Threat modeling helps organizations proactively address security risks.

Patch management is the process of regularly applying updates and patches to software and systems to fix known vulnerabilities. Unpatched systems are susceptible to exploitation by attackers. Effective patch management is critical for maintaining the integrity and security of a network.

Social engineering is a non-technical attack vector that exploits human psychology to manipulate individuals into revealing sensitive information or performing actions that compromise security. Understanding social engineering tactics and educating users about them is essential for countering this pervasive threat.

Authentication is the process of verifying the identity of users or systems. Effective authentication methods, such as strong passwords, multi-factor authentication (MFA), and biometrics, are fundamental for ensuring that only authorized entities gain access to network resources.

Authorization, often coupled with authentication, defines what actions or resources an authenticated user or system is permitted to access. RBAC is a common authorization model that assigns specific roles and permissions to users based on their job functions. Comprehending authorization mechanisms is crucial for controlling access effectively.

Incident response is a structured approach to addressing and mitigating security incidents. Understanding incident response procedures, including detection, containment, eradication, and recovery, is vital for minimizing the impact of security breaches.

Security policies and procedures establish guidelines and best practices for network security. These documents help organizations define their security posture, set expectations for users, and ensure compliance with legal and regulatory requirements.

Security awareness and training programs educate users and employees about security threats and best practices.

A well-informed workforce is an essential defense against social engineering and other security risks.

Network monitoring involves the continuous observation of network traffic and system behavior. Monitoring tools and techniques help identify abnormal or suspicious activities, allowing organizations to respond promptly to potential security incidents.

Threat intelligence is information about emerging threats, vulnerabilities, and attacker tactics, techniques, and procedures (TTPs). Leveraging threat intelligence sources helps organizations stay informed about evolving security risks.

Risk assessment is the process of identifying and evaluating potential security risks to prioritize mitigation efforts. Understanding risk assessment methodologies assists organizations in making informed decisions about security investments and resource allocation.

Compliance standards, such as the Payment Card Industry Data Security Standard (PCI DSS) or the General Data Protection Regulation (GDPR), establish security requirements that organizations must follow. Compliance with these standards is essential for legal and regulatory reasons.

Network security concepts are foundational to creating a robust and effective security posture. To navigate the complex landscape of network security, individuals and organizations must grasp these fundamental principles, technologies, and practices to protect their valuable assets and sensitive data effectively.

Security in network architecture is of paramount importance in the digital age, where the reliance on interconnected systems and data sharing is ubiquitous. Networks are the backbone of modern organizations, facilitating communication, data exchange, and collaboration, making their security a critical consideration.

The digital transformation has brought numerous benefits, but it has also exposed networks to an ever-growing array of threats. As organizations rely more on technology, the potential impact of security breaches becomes more severe.

One crucial aspect of network security is data protection. Networks often transmit sensitive and confidential information, such as financial data, personal records, and intellectual property. Without robust security measures in place, this data can be intercepted, accessed, or manipulated by malicious actors.

To address this concern, encryption technologies play a pivotal role. Encryption ensures that data remains confidential during transmission, even if intercepted. The use of encryption protocols such as SSL/TLS for securing web traffic or IPsec for virtual private networks (VPNs) is integral to modern network security.

Another aspect of network security is access control, which dictates who can access specific resources and what actions they can perform. Unauthorized access can lead to data breaches, unauthorized modifications, and system disruptions. Effective access control mechanisms, such as role-based access control (RBAC) or least privilege principle, help organizations enforce security policies.

Moreover, network segmentation is a fundamental security strategy. Segmenting a network involves dividing it into smaller, isolated segments or subnetworks. This limits lateral movement for attackers within a network and reduces the impact of a breach. Segmentation ensures that even if one part of the network is compromised, other segments remain secure.

Firewalls are key components of network architecture, acting as barriers between trusted internal networks and untrusted external networks, typically the internet. Firewalls use a set of rules to determine which network traffic is allowed or denied. Implementing firewalls strategically is vital for controlling inbound and outbound traffic, mitigating threats, and enforcing security policies.

Intrusion detection and prevention systems (IDS/IPS) are essential elements of network security. These systems monitor network traffic for suspicious activities or patterns. An IDS identifies potential security threats, while an IPS takes action to block or mitigate those threats. IDS/IPS solutions are indispensable for early threat detection and response.

For organizations, securing the perimeter of their network is essential. This involves implementing measures such as firewalls, intrusion detection, and access controls to protect against external threats. However, the modern threat landscape includes insider threats, which necessitates a focus on internal network security as well.

Network monitoring plays a critical role in both threat detection and performance optimization. Monitoring tools and techniques help identify abnormal or suspicious activities, allowing organizations to respond promptly to potential security incidents. Additionally, monitoring assists in identifying and resolving network performance issues.

Authentication is a core component of network security. It involves verifying the identity of users or systems before granting access to network resources. Strong authentication methods, such as multi-factor authentication (MFA) or biometrics, are essential for ensuring that only authorized entities gain access.

Beyond authentication, authorization defines what actions or resources an authenticated user or system is permitted to access. Implementing proper authorization mechanisms is crucial for controlling access effectively.

Vulnerability management is an ongoing process in network security. It involves identifying, assessing, and prioritizing vulnerabilities within the network infrastructure. Regularly applying patches and updates to software and systems is essential to address known vulnerabilities.

Threat modeling is a systematic approach to identifying and mitigating potential threats to a network or system. It involves evaluating vulnerabilities, assessing the likelihood and impact of threats, and prioritizing security measures. Threat modeling helps organizations proactively address security risks.

Network security is not solely about technology; it also involves people and processes. Security awareness and training programs educate users and employees about security threats and best practices. A well-informed workforce is an essential defense against social engineering and other security risks.

Incident response is a structured approach to addressing and mitigating security incidents. Understanding incident response procedures, including detection, containment, eradication, and recovery, is vital for minimizing the impact of security breaches.

Compliance standards, such as the Payment Card Industry Data Security Standard (PCI DSS) or the General Data Protection Regulation (GDPR), establish security requirements that organizations must follow. Compliance with these standards is essential for legal and regulatory reasons.

The importance of security in network architecture cannot be overstated. A breach in network security can result in financial losses, damage to reputation, legal liabilities, and even the compromise of national security. Protecting the integrity, confidentiality, and availability of networked data and systems is a collective responsibility that requires continuous vigilance, education, and adaptation to evolving threats.

In summary, security in network architecture is not a standalone consideration but an integral part of an organization's overall strategy. The interconnected nature of modern networks demands a comprehensive and proactive approach to security. By implementing robust security measures, organizations can safeguard their data, protect their assets, and ensure the trust and confidence of their stakeholders.

Chapter 2: NMAP for Threat Assessment

NMAP is a versatile and powerful network scanning tool that has gained recognition not only for its utility in network administration but also as an essential tool for threat assessment and vulnerability identification.

In the realm of threat assessment, NMAP serves a dual purpose – it can be used to evaluate the security posture of a network from an external perspective, and it can be employed internally to discover and remediate vulnerabilities before they are exploited by malicious actors.

One of the primary functions of NMAP in threat assessment is reconnaissance. Reconnaissance is the process of gathering information about a target network, and it is often the first step taken by potential attackers. NMAP assists in this phase by providing a comprehensive view of the network's exposed services, open ports, and potential entry points.

When assessing external threats, organizations can deploy NMAP to conduct port scanning and service identification on their publicly accessible servers. This process helps identify which services are running on these servers and which ports are open. An example CLI command for this purpose is:

shell

nmap -p- -T4 -oN scan_results.txt target_domain_or_IP

In this command:

-p- instructs NMAP to scan all 65,535 ports.

-T4 specifies the timing template to use, balancing between speed and reliability.

-oN scan_results.txt directs NMAP to save the scan results to a text file.

target_domain_or_IP should be replaced with the domain or IP address of the target.

Once the scan is completed, the organization can analyze the results to determine which ports and services are exposed to the internet. Any unexpected or unnecessary services can be further scrutinized and potentially secured or removed to reduce the attack surface.

Additionally, NMAP's version detection capabilities allow organizations to ascertain not only which services are running but also their exact versions. This information is crucial because outdated or unpatched software may contain known vulnerabilities that can be exploited by attackers.

To perform version detection, you can use a command like this:

shell

```
nmap -sV -oN version_results.txt target_domain_or_IP
```

In this command:

-sV enables version detection.

-oN version_results.txt saves the results to a text file.

target_domain_or_IP should be replaced with the target's domain or IP address.

The output will include a list of services and their corresponding versions, allowing organizations to prioritize patching or upgrading vulnerable software.

Internally, NMAP can also be a valuable asset in threat assessment by scanning the organization's internal network for vulnerabilities. By running periodic scans on internal subnets and devices, administrators can identify open ports, misconfigured services, and potential weaknesses that need attention.

A typical internal network scan with NMAP may look like this:

shell

```
nmap -p 1-65535 -T4 -oN internal_scan_results.txt internal_subnet
```

In this command:

-p 1-65535 specifies scanning all ports.

-T4 sets the timing template to a balanced speed and reliability setting.

-oN internal_scan_results.txt directs NMAP to save the results to a text file.

internal_subnet should be replaced with the subnet range to scan.

Regular internal scans help organizations maintain a proactive approach to security, as they can detect and rectify vulnerabilities before they are exploited by internal or external threats.

Furthermore, NMAP's scripting engine, known as the NMAP Scripting Engine (NSE), enhances its capabilities for threat assessment. NSE scripts can automate various tasks, including vulnerability scanning, service enumeration, and even security assessments tailored to specific applications or protocols.

For example, an organization can utilize NSE scripts to perform a script-based vulnerability scan like this:

shell

```
nmap --script vuln -oN vuln_scan_results.txt target_domain_or_IP
```

In this command:

--script vuln instructs NMAP to use scripts that focus on vulnerability detection.

-oN vuln_scan_results.txt saves the results to a text file.

target_domain_or_IP should be replaced with the target's domain or IP address.

The NSE scripts perform checks for known vulnerabilities in the target's services and applications, providing organizations with valuable insights into their security posture.

In summary, NMAP's versatility, speed, and accuracy make it an indispensable tool for threat assessment in today's interconnected and dynamic digital landscape. Whether used externally to assess internet-facing assets or internally to monitor the security of internal networks, NMAP provides organizations with the means to identify vulnerabilities, reduce attack surfaces, and proactively protect against threats. By leveraging its port scanning, version detection, internal network scanning, and NSE scripting capabilities, organizations can enhance their overall security posture and mitigate potential risks effectively.

Identifying vulnerabilities is a critical aspect of maintaining a secure network environment, and NMAP proves to be a valuable tool in this endeavor. Vulnerabilities are weaknesses or flaws in a system or application that can be exploited by attackers to gain unauthorized access, disrupt services, or steal data. The process of identifying vulnerabilities is an essential part of proactive security measures.

NMAP offers several features and techniques that assist in identifying vulnerabilities within a network. One of its primary functions in this regard is conducting comprehensive vulnerability scans to pinpoint potential weaknesses. These scans are typically categorized as either credentialed or non-credentialed scans.

A non-credentialed scan, also known as an external scan, is performed without the need for valid credentials, making it ideal for assessing the security of internet-facing systems. In this type of scan, NMAP primarily focuses on open ports, services, and their versions. It can provide information about which services may be susceptible to known vulnerabilities.

An example of a non-credentialed scan command using NMAP is as follows:

shell

```
nmap -p 1-65535 -T4 -A -oN external_scan_results.txt target_domain_or_IP
```

In this command:

-p 1-65535 specifies scanning all ports.

-T4 sets the timing template to a balanced speed and reliability setting.

-A enables OS detection, version detection, script scanning, and traceroute.

-oN external_scan_results.txt directs NMAP to save the results to a text file.

target_domain_or_IP should be replaced with the target's domain or IP address.

The results of such a scan can help organizations identify potential vulnerabilities related to open ports and services. For example, if NMAP detects an outdated or unpatched version of a service, it may be susceptible to known exploits, which should prompt immediate remediation efforts.

On the other hand, credentialed scans, also known as internal scans, require valid credentials to access the target systems. These scans offer a more in-depth assessment of vulnerabilities within the network, as they can inspect the internal configuration and software of devices.

Credentialed scans can be particularly valuable for identifying vulnerabilities on servers, workstations, and other networked devices within an organization. NMAP, when used with the appropriate credentials, can perform authenticated scans to gather detailed information about the target systems' configuration and installed software.

To conduct an authenticated scan with NMAP, you can use a command like this:

shell

nmap -p 1-65535 -T4 -A -oN authenticated_scan_results.txt -iL target_list.txt

In this command:

-p 1-65535 specifies scanning all ports.

-T4 sets the timing template to a balanced speed and reliability setting.

-A enables OS detection, version detection, script scanning, and traceroute.

-oN authenticated_scan_results.txt directs NMAP to save the results to a text file.

-iL target_list.txt reads a list of target IP addresses or hostnames from the specified file.

Authenticated scans allow NMAP to gather extensive information about the target systems, such as installed software versions, patches, and configurations. This data is invaluable for identifying vulnerabilities and ensuring that systems are up-to-date with security patches.

Another useful feature of NMAP for identifying vulnerabilities is its scripting engine, the NMAP Scripting Engine (NSE). NSE provides a collection of scripts that can be used to automate vulnerability checks and security assessments on target systems.

For instance, NSE scripts can be utilized to perform a script-based vulnerability scan on a target system. Here is an example of a command that leverages NSE scripts for vulnerability detection:

shell

nmap --script vuln -oN vulnerability_scan_results.txt target_domain_or_IP

In this command:

--script vuln instructs NMAP to use scripts specifically focused on vulnerability detection.

-oN vulnerability_scan_results.txt directs NMAP to save the results to a text file.

target_domain_or_IP should be replaced with the target's domain or IP address.

The NSE scripts perform checks for known vulnerabilities in the target's services and applications, providing organizations with actionable information to remediate vulnerabilities promptly.

Additionally, NMAP's scripting capabilities extend to custom script development. Organizations can create their own NSE scripts tailored to their specific applications or environments. Writing custom NSE scripts allows security teams to assess unique vulnerabilities that may not be covered by publicly available scripts.

In summary, identifying vulnerabilities within a network is an ongoing and essential process for maintaining security. NMAP, with its port scanning, version detection, authenticated scanning, and NSE scripting capabilities, proves to be a valuable asset in this effort. By conducting vulnerability scans, organizations can pinpoint weaknesses in their systems and applications, prioritize remediation efforts, and fortify their network against potential threats. Moreover, the flexibility of NMAP allows security professionals to adapt and extend its functionality to address specific vulnerabilities and security concerns unique to their environments.

Chapter 3: Firewall and ACL Analysis

Analyzing firewall rules is a critical aspect of network security, and NMAP can serve as a valuable tool for this purpose. Firewalls act as barriers between trusted internal networks and potentially untrusted external networks, such as the internet. They use a set of rules to determine which network traffic is allowed or denied, making them a fundamental component of network security.

Firewall rules dictate how traffic flows through the network and which services or ports are accessible from different sources. These rules are configured to enforce security policies, control access, and mitigate threats. However, over time, firewall rules can become complex and convoluted, potentially introducing vulnerabilities or misconfigurations.

Analyzing firewall rules with NMAP involves assessing the effectiveness and security of these rules. It aims to identify potential weaknesses or inconsistencies that could be exploited by attackers.

NMAP can perform firewall rule analysis by conducting port scans and service identification, both from an external and internal perspective.

To analyze firewall rules from an external perspective, organizations can deploy NMAP to scan their publicly accessible servers and services. This external scan simulates how attackers would approach the network and helps identify which services are exposed to the internet.

An example of an NMAP command for an external firewall rule analysis is as follows:

shell

nmap -p 1-65535 -T4 -A -oN external_firewall_analysis.txt target_domain_or_IP

In this command:

-p 1-65535 specifies scanning all ports.

-T4 sets the timing template to a balanced speed and reliability setting.

-A enables OS detection, version detection, script scanning, and traceroute.

-oN external_firewall_analysis.txt directs NMAP to save the results to a text file.

target_domain_or_IP should be replaced with the target's domain or IP address.

The results of this scan reveal which ports are open and which services are running on the publicly accessible servers. By comparing these findings to the organization's firewall rules, security teams can ensure that only the necessary services are exposed to the internet and that unauthorized access attempts are thwarted.

Additionally, NMAP can assess the effectiveness of ingress and egress firewall rules by conducting internal scans. These scans simulate an attacker who has already breached the perimeter and is trying to move laterally within the network.

To perform an internal firewall rule analysis, organizations can use NMAP to scan internal subnets and devices. This helps identify any open ports or services that should not be accessible from certain parts of the network.

An example of an NMAP command for internal firewall rule analysis is as follows:

shell

nmap -p 1-65535 -T4 -A -oN internal_firewall_analysis.txt internal_subnet

In this command:

-p 1-65535 specifies scanning all ports.

-T4 sets the timing template to a balanced speed and reliability setting.

-A enables OS detection, version detection, script scanning, and traceroute.

-oN internal_firewall_analysis.txt directs NMAP to save the results to a text file.

internal_subnet should be replaced with the subnet range to scan.

The results of this scan can help organizations verify that their internal firewall rules are effectively segregating and isolating network segments to prevent lateral movement by attackers.

In addition to traditional port scanning, NMAP's scripting engine, the NMAP Scripting Engine (NSE), can be a valuable asset for firewall rule analysis. NSE scripts can be utilized to automate the testing of specific firewall rules and configurations.

For example, NSE scripts can simulate specific types of network traffic and assess whether firewall rules are correctly blocking or allowing that traffic. This helps organizations verify that their firewall rules align with their intended security policies.

To leverage NSE scripts for firewall rule analysis, an organization can use commands like the following:

shell

nmap --script firewall-scan -oN firewall_script_analysis.txt target_domain_or_IP

In this command:

--script firewall-scan specifies the use of NSE scripts designed for firewall analysis.

-oN firewall_script_analysis.txt directs NMAP to save the results to a text file.

target_domain_or_IP should be replaced with the target's domain or IP address.

The NSE scripts provide detailed insights into firewall rule effectiveness, helping organizations identify potential weaknesses or misconfigurations that need attention.

In summary, analyzing firewall rules with NMAP is a crucial aspect of network security. Firewalls play a pivotal role in protecting networks from external threats and controlling traffic within the network. Regular analysis using NMAP's port scanning, service identification, and NSE scripting capabilities allows organizations to ensure that their firewall rules align with their security policies and that potential vulnerabilities or misconfigurations are promptly addressed. By maintaining robust firewall rules, organizations can strengthen their overall network security and reduce the risk of unauthorized access or data breaches.

Assessing Access Control Lists (ACLs) is a crucial task in network security management, as these lists define which users or systems are allowed or denied access to specific resources. Access control is fundamental for maintaining the confidentiality, integrity, and availability of data and services within a network. ACLs are a set of rules that determine what traffic is permitted or blocked at various network layers, including routers, switches, and firewalls.

Evaluating ACLs involves reviewing and analyzing these rules to ensure they align with an organization's security policies and are configured correctly. Mistakes or misconfigurations in ACLs can lead to security vulnerabilities, unauthorized access, and network disruptions.

One of the primary tools for assessing ACLs is NMAP, a versatile network scanning and auditing tool. NMAP can be used to perform ACL analysis by simulating network traffic and testing how ACL rules handle different types of packets.

To assess ACLs using NMAP, security professionals can initiate scans that involve sending packets with specific characteristics and observing the responses. NMAP can assist in identifying whether ACLs permit or deny certain types of traffic, which is crucial for verifying that access restrictions are working as intended.

An example NMAP command for assessing ACLs involves performing a simple ping scan against a target network to determine if ICMP (Internet Control Message Protocol) traffic is allowed or blocked:

shell

nmap -sn -PS target_IP_or_subnet

In this command:

-sn instructs NMAP to perform a ping scan without further probing.

-PS specifies the TCP ping scan, which sends TCP packets to probe for open ports.

target_IP_or_subnet should be replaced with the target IP address or subnet to assess.

If the ping scan results show that ICMP traffic is blocked or filtered, it indicates that the ACLs are likely configured to deny ICMP requests, which can be a deliberate security measure to prevent certain types of network reconnaissance.

Conversely, if the scan successfully receives ICMP responses, it suggests that ICMP traffic is allowed by the ACLs.

Beyond ICMP, NMAP can be used to assess ACLs for specific services or ports. For instance, if an organization wants to verify that only authorized systems can access a web server on port 80, NMAP can be employed to test the accessibility of that port.

Here is an example NMAP command for assessing ACLs by scanning port 80:

shell

nmap -p 80 target_IP_or_subnet

In this command:

-p 80 specifies scanning only port 80.

target_IP_or_subnet should be replaced with the target IP address or subnet to assess.

The scan results will reveal whether port 80 is open and accessible, indicating that traffic to this port is permitted by the ACLs.

Moreover, NMAP's scripting engine, the NMAP Scripting Engine (NSE), enhances ACL assessment capabilities by offering specialized scripts designed to probe for specific ACL-related issues.

For instance, NMAP includes an NSE script called **firewalk** that can be used to determine which ACL rules permit or deny traffic to a specific host and port.

Here is an example NMAP command that employs the **firewalk** script to assess ACLs for a target host and port:

shell

nmap --script firewalk -p 80 target_IP_or_subnet

In this command:

--script firewalk specifies the use of the **firewalk** NSE script.

-p 80 defines the target port (in this case, port 80).

target_IP_or_subnet should be replaced with the target IP address or subnet to assess.

The **firewalk** script will simulate traceroute-like probes to determine whether packets can traverse ACLs to reach the specified host and port. It provides valuable insights into the ACL rules that impact network traffic to the target.

In summary, assessing Access Control Lists (ACLs) is a critical aspect of network security management. These lists define access permissions and restrictions within a network, and errors or misconfigurations can lead to security vulnerabilities. NMAP is a valuable tool for ACL assessment, as it allows security professionals to simulate network traffic and test how ACL rules handle different types of packets. By using NMAP's scanning capabilities, such as ping scans and port scans, along with NSE scripts like **firewalk**, organizations can verify that their ACLs align with their security policies and effectively control access to network resources. Regular ACL assessments are essential for maintaining a robust and secure network infrastructure.

Chapter 4: Securing Open Ports and Services

Best practices for port security are essential to safeguarding network resources and protecting against unauthorized access and potential security breaches. Port security refers to the measures and configurations applied to network ports to control the flow of data and ensure that only authorized devices can connect and communicate through these ports.

One fundamental principle of port security is to limit and control access. This involves configuring network devices, such as switches and routers, to prevent unauthorized devices from connecting to network ports. Unauthorized access can introduce security risks and vulnerabilities, making it essential to employ strict access controls.

A common technique for implementing port security is the use of IEEE 802.1X authentication. IEEE 802.1X is a standard that defines port-based network access control, allowing devices to authenticate before they are granted access to the network. This authentication process can use various methods, such as username and password or digital certificates.

To deploy IEEE 802.1X authentication, network administrators need to configure network devices, such as switches, to enable this feature on the relevant ports. For example, on a Cisco Catalyst switch, the following CLI commands can be used to enable IEEE 802.1X authentication on an Ethernet port:

shell

interface FastEthernet0/1 switchport mode access authentication port-control auto

In this configuration:

interface FastEthernet0/1 specifies the network port to be configured.

switchport mode access sets the port mode to access, which is required for IEEE 802.1X.

authentication port-control auto enables automatic IEEE 802.1X port control.

With IEEE 802.1X authentication enabled, only devices that successfully authenticate can use the network port, preventing unauthorized access.

Another crucial aspect of port security is MAC address filtering. This technique involves specifying which MAC addresses are allowed or denied access to a network port. By maintaining a list of authorized MAC addresses, network administrators can ensure that only trusted devices can connect to specific ports.

To configure MAC address filtering on a Cisco switch port, administrators can use the following CLI commands:

shell

interface   FastEthernet0/1   switchport   port-security switchport port-security violation restrict switchport port-security mac-address sticky

In this configuration:

interface FastEthernet0/1 specifies the network port to be configured.

switchport port-security enables port security on the port.

switchport port-security violation restrict configures the port to restrict unauthorized access without shutting down the port.

switchport port-security mac-address sticky enables the sticky MAC address feature, which allows the switch to learn and remember authorized MAC addresses dynamically.

By using MAC address filtering, network administrators can enforce tighter control over who can connect to specific network ports.

Additionally, it's essential to employ physical security measures to protect network ports. Physical security includes measures such as locking network closets or cabinets, using secure cable connectors, and installing tamper-evident seals to prevent physical tampering or unauthorized access to network ports.

Furthermore, regularly reviewing and updating port security configurations is a crucial best practice. Network environments can evolve, and new devices may need access to certain ports, while others should be restricted. Periodic audits of port security configurations ensure that access controls remain aligned with current network requirements and security policies.

When reviewing port security configurations, administrators should also pay attention to any security alerts or logs generated by network devices. These logs can provide valuable insights into potential security incidents or unauthorized access attempts. Analyzing log data helps identify security weaknesses and allows for timely response and mitigation.

In summary, implementing best practices for port security is essential for maintaining a secure and resilient network infrastructure. Controlling access through IEEE 802.1X authentication and MAC address filtering, ensuring physical security, and regularly reviewing and updating configurations are all vital components of effective port security. By following these practices, organizations can reduce the risk of unauthorized access, protect sensitive data, and strengthen their overall network security posture. Port security is an ongoing effort that requires vigilance and adaptability to address evolving security threats and network requirements.

Securing services and applications is a critical aspect of modern information security practices. As organizations rely more on digital services and applications for their operations, the need to protect these assets from various threats becomes paramount. This chapter explores the strategies and techniques for securing services and applications effectively.

One fundamental principle of securing services and applications is to follow the principle of least privilege. This means that users, services, or applications should only have the minimum permissions necessary to perform their tasks. By reducing unnecessary privileges, organizations can limit the potential impact of security breaches.

To implement the principle of least privilege, organizations can employ access control mechanisms, such as role-based access control (RBAC) or attribute-based access control (ABAC). These mechanisms allow organizations to define who can access specific services or applications and what actions they can perform.

For example, in a Linux-based environment, administrators can use the **chmod** command to set file permissions for a web application configuration file:

shell

```
chmod 600 config.ini
```

In this command:

chmod is the command for changing file permissions.

600 sets the file permissions to read and write only for the owner.

This command restricts access to the configuration file to the owner, ensuring that sensitive information is not exposed to unauthorized users.

Additionally, organizations should regularly update and patch their services and applications to address known vulnerabilities. Vulnerabilities can be exploited by attackers to compromise systems and gain unauthorized access. By applying security patches promptly, organizations can reduce the attack surface and mitigate the risk of exploitation.

To update packages in a Linux-based system, administrators can use package management commands such as **apt-get** or **yum**:

shell

sudo apt-get update sudo apt-get upgrade

In these commands:

sudo is used to run the commands with superuser privileges.

apt-get update refreshes the package list.

apt-get upgrade installs available updates.

Regularly monitoring and auditing services and applications is another essential security practice. Organizations should employ intrusion detection systems (IDS) and intrusion prevention systems (IPS) to detect and respond to suspicious activities. Additionally, log files should be generated and reviewed regularly to identify potential security incidents or abnormal behaviors.

For example, the **tail** command can be used to view the last few lines of a log file:

shell

tail -n 100 /var/log/application.log

In this command:

tail displays the last few lines of a file.

-n 100 specifies displaying the last 100 lines.

/var/log/application.log is the path to the log file.

By monitoring log files, organizations can identify patterns of unauthorized access, suspicious activities, or security breaches and take appropriate action.

Authentication and authorization mechanisms are crucial components of securing services and applications. Authentication ensures that users or entities are who they claim to be, while authorization defines what actions they are allowed to perform.

Implementing strong authentication methods, such as multi-factor authentication (MFA), enhances security by requiring users to provide multiple forms of verification, such as a password and a one-time code sent to their mobile device.

To enable MFA for a web application, organizations can integrate authentication libraries and services, such as OAuth or OpenID Connect. These standards allow users to authenticate using their existing credentials with third-party identity providers like Google or Microsoft.

Incorporating MFA into the authentication process adds an extra layer of security, reducing the risk of unauthorized access.

Authorization mechanisms, on the other hand, determine what resources or functionalities users or entities can access. RBAC and ABAC are commonly used authorization models, with RBAC defining roles and permissions and ABAC considering attributes and conditions.

In cloud environments, organizations can use identity and access management (IAM) policies to control access to services and resources. IAM policies specify who can perform actions on specific resources and under what conditions.

For instance, in Amazon Web Services (AWS), an IAM policy might grant read-only access to a specific S3 bucket:
json

```json
{ "Version": "2012-10-17", "Statement": [ { "Effect": "Allow", "Action": "s3:GetObject", "Resource": "arn:aws:s3:::example-bucket/*", "Condition": { "IpAddress": { "aws:SourceIp": "192.168.1.0/24" } } } ] }
```

In this policy:

"Effect": "Allow" specifies that the action is allowed.

"Action": "s3:GetObject" defines the action to get objects from the S3 bucket.

"Resource": "arn:aws:s3:::example-bucket/*" specifies the resource, which is the S3 bucket.

"Condition" sets the condition for allowing access based on the source IP address.

By utilizing IAM policies, organizations can enforce fine-grained access controls for their cloud resources and services.

Encrypting data is another vital aspect of securing services and applications. Data encryption ensures that data in transit and data at rest are protected from eavesdropping and unauthorized access.

Transport Layer Security (TLS) and Secure Sockets Layer (SSL) protocols are widely used to encrypt data in transit. By configuring web servers to use TLS or SSL certificates, organizations can secure data transmission between clients and servers.

To enable TLS on an Apache web server, administrators can use the following CLI commands:

shell

```shell
sudo a2enmod ssl sudo systemctl restart apache2
```

In these commands:

sudo a2enmod ssl enables the SSL module for Apache.

sudo systemctl restart apache2 restarts the Apache service to apply the changes.

Encrypting data at rest involves using encryption algorithms to protect data stored on disks or databases. Organizations can use encryption tools and technologies, such as LUKS (Linux Unified Key Setup) for disk encryption or database encryption plugins, to safeguard sensitive data.

In Linux-based systems, LUKS can be used to encrypt a disk partition:

shell

```
sudo cryptsetup luksFormat /dev/sdX sudo cryptsetup luksOpen /dev/sdX encrypted_volume sudo mkfs.ext4 /dev/mapper/encrypted_volume
```

In these commands:

sudo cryptsetup luksFormat /dev/sdX initializes the LUKS encryption on the specified disk.

sudo cryptsetup luksOpen /dev/sdX encrypted_volume opens the encrypted volume.

sudo mkfs.ext4 /dev/mapper/encrypted_volume creates a file system on the encrypted volume.

By applying encryption techniques, organizations can protect data from unauthorized access, even if physical devices are compromised.

Lastly, organizations should have an incident response plan in place to address security breaches or incidents promptly. An incident response plan outlines the steps and procedures to follow when a security event occurs.

The plan should include a clear escalation process, contact information for relevant parties, and predefined actions to contain and mitigate the incident. Regularly testing and updating the incident response plan ensures its effectiveness when needed.

In summary, securing services and applications is a multifaceted process that requires a combination of access control, monitoring, authentication, authorization, encryption, and incident response. Organizations must continually assess and adapt their security measures to address evolving threats and vulnerabilities in an ever-changing digital landscape. By implementing these security practices, organizations can reduce the risk of security breaches and protect their valuable assets and data.

Chapter 5: Intrusion Detection and Prevention

Implementing intrusion detection with NMAP is a valuable strategy to enhance network security. Intrusion detection involves the monitoring of network traffic and system activities to identify and respond to potential security threats or suspicious behavior.

NMAP, known primarily as a network scanning tool, can also be utilized for intrusion detection purposes. By leveraging its network discovery and mapping capabilities, NMAP can help organizations detect unauthorized devices, suspicious network traffic patterns, and potential vulnerabilities.

One of the primary techniques for implementing intrusion detection with NMAP is through the use of custom scripts and the NMAP Scripting Engine (NSE). The NSE allows security professionals to develop and deploy custom scripts that extend NMAP's functionality and enable specific intrusion detection tasks.

To create a custom NMAP script for intrusion detection, security professionals can utilize a programming language like Lua, which is supported by NSE. They can develop scripts that perform tasks such as monitoring network traffic, identifying unusual patterns, or conducting vulnerability checks.

For example, a custom NMAP script might be created to detect and log any network traffic originating from or directed at a specific IP address or range of IP addresses. The script can be designed to continuously monitor the network and generate alerts when suspicious traffic is detected.

Here is a simple example of a custom NMAP script written in Lua that logs incoming network connections to a specific IP address:

lua

```lua
local ip_to_monitor = "192.168.1.100" function action(host,
port) if host.ip == ip_to_monitor then print("Suspicious
connection from " .. host.ip .. " to port " .. port.number) --
Additional actions can be taken, such as sending alerts or
blocking the connection. end end
```

In this script:

ip_to_monitor is the IP address that the script is monitoring.

The **action** function is called whenever a new host and port combination is discovered by NMAP.

If the discovered host's IP matches the one being monitored, the script logs a suspicious connection.

Custom NMAP scripts like this can be executed alongside regular NMAP scans to provide real-time intrusion detection capabilities.

Additionally, NMAP's ability to perform version detection can be leveraged for intrusion detection. Version detection involves analyzing the responses from network services to determine the software and its version running on a target host.

Security professionals can use NMAP's version detection to identify known vulnerabilities associated with specific software versions. By scanning a network and comparing discovered software versions to vulnerability databases, organizations can identify potential risks and vulnerabilities.

For instance, an NMAP scan can be executed with version detection enabled to identify the software and versions running on network hosts:

shell

```shell
nmap -sV -oN scan_results.txt 192.168.1.0/24
```

In this command:

-sV instructs NMAP to perform version detection.

-oN scan_results.txt specifies the output file for the scan results.

192.168.1.0/24 is the target network range to scan.

Once the scan is complete, the results can be compared to known vulnerability databases or security advisories to assess potential risks.

Furthermore, NMAP can be integrated into a broader intrusion detection and prevention system (IDPS) architecture. IDPS solutions combine various technologies and tools, including NMAP, to detect and respond to security threats effectively.

In an IDPS environment, NMAP can be used for periodic network scans to establish a baseline of normal network behavior. Any deviations from this baseline can trigger alerts or actions, indicating potential intrusions or security incidents.

For example, if NMAP scans detect new or unknown devices on the network, the IDPS system can automatically initiate further investigation or isolation measures.

Additionally, NMAP can be employed in conjunction with log analysis tools and security information and event management (SIEM) systems. The combination of network scanning data from NMAP and log data from various sources can provide a comprehensive view of network activities, aiding in intrusion detection and analysis.

In summary, implementing intrusion detection with NMAP involves utilizing its network scanning capabilities and custom scripts to monitor network traffic, identify vulnerabilities, and detect suspicious activities. NMAP's flexibility and extensibility through the NMAP Scripting Engine make it a valuable tool for enhancing network security. When integrated into a broader security infrastructure, NMAP can contribute to a robust intrusion detection and prevention strategy, helping organizations proactively protect their networks from potential threats and security breaches.

Preventing intrusions using NMAP requires a proactive approach to network security. While NMAP is primarily known as a network scanning tool, it can also be used as a valuable component of an intrusion prevention strategy.

One of the key ways to prevent intrusions using NMAP is by conducting regular vulnerability assessments. NMAP's powerful scanning capabilities allow organizations to identify weaknesses and potential entry points that attackers could exploit.

To perform a basic vulnerability assessment using NMAP, organizations can run a comprehensive scan of their network, including all hosts and open ports. This scan provides valuable information about the services and software versions running on network devices.

For example, the following NMAP command scans a target network and outputs the results to a file:

shell

```
nmap    -A    -T4    -oN    vulnerability_assessment.txt
192.168.1.0/24
```

In this command:

-A instructs NMAP to perform aggressive scanning, including service and version detection.

-T4 sets the scan speed to a reasonably fast rate.

-oN vulnerability_assessment.txt specifies the output file for the scan results.

192.168.1.0/24 is the target network range to scan.

By analyzing the results of the vulnerability assessment, organizations can prioritize security efforts and address potential vulnerabilities before attackers can exploit them.

Another technique for preventing intrusions with NMAP is network segmentation. Network segmentation involves dividing a network into smaller, isolated segments or VLANs (Virtual Local Area Networks) to limit an attacker's lateral movement within the network.

Organizations can use NMAP to scan their network and identify areas where segmentation is needed. By understanding the network's layout and potential weak points, security professionals can recommend and implement segmentation measures.

For instance, an NMAP scan may reveal that sensitive servers and user workstations share the same network segment. To improve security, organizations can implement network segmentation by isolating these devices into separate VLANs, effectively containing potential intrusions.

Implementing network segmentation typically involves configuring switches and routers to enforce access controls and isolate traffic between VLANs. For example, in a Cisco networking environment, administrators can use the following CLI commands to create VLANs and assign ports: shell

configure terminal vlan 10 name Servers exit vlan 20 name Workstations exit interface GigabitEthernet0/1 switchport access vlan 10 exit interface GigabitEthernet0/2 switchport access vlan 20 exit

In these commands:

configure terminal enters configuration mode on the switch.

vlan 10 creates a VLAN with the ID 10.

name Servers assigns a name to the VLAN.

exit exits VLAN configuration mode.

interface GigabitEthernet0/1 enters configuration mode for a specific interface.

switchport access vlan 10 assigns the interface to VLAN 10.

exit exits interface configuration mode.

By isolating sensitive resources in separate VLANs, organizations can minimize the risk of lateral movement and unauthorized access in the event of an intrusion.

Additionally, NMAP can be employed as a tool for monitoring network traffic for signs of intrusion. Organizations can set up NMAP scans as part of an intrusion detection system (IDS) to periodically assess network health and detect anomalies.

For instance, scheduled NMAP scans can be configured to run at specific intervals to monitor the network's state and verify that no unauthorized devices or services have appeared. Any deviations from the expected scan results can trigger alerts or further investigation.

To automate scheduled NMAP scans, organizations can create scripts or use task scheduling tools like cron (on Unix-based systems) or Task Scheduler (on Windows) to execute NMAP commands at predetermined times.

For example, a Unix-based organization could create a cron job to run an NMAP scan every night at midnight:

shell

```
0 0 * * * /usr/bin/nmap -T4 -oN nightly_scan.txt 192.168.1.0/24
```

In this cron job:

0 0 * * * specifies the schedule (midnight every day).

/usr/bin/nmap is the path to the NMAP executable.

-T4 sets the scan speed.

-oN nightly_scan.txt specifies the output file.

192.168.1.0/24 is the target network range.

By incorporating NMAP into an IDS, organizations can continuously monitor their network's security posture and detect intrusions or suspicious activities in real-time.

Another aspect of intrusion prevention using NMAP involves the monitoring and analysis of NMAP scan data. Organizations can collect and analyze NMAP scan results to identify patterns, trends, or unusual behaviors that may indicate potential threats.

Log analysis tools and security information and event management (SIEM) systems can be used to process and correlate NMAP scan data with other security events and logs. This integration enables security professionals to gain insights into network activities and identify potential intrusion attempts.

In summary, preventing intrusions using NMAP requires a combination of vulnerability assessments, network segmentation, scheduled scans for anomaly detection, and data analysis. NMAP's versatility as a network scanning tool makes it a valuable asset in enhancing network security. When used as part of a broader intrusion prevention strategy, NMAP can help organizations proactively identify and mitigate potential threats, reducing the risk of security breaches and unauthorized access to their networks.

Chapter 6: Hardening Network Devices

Strengthening network device security is a critical aspect of overall network security. Network devices, including routers, switches, firewalls, and access points, play a central role in managing and controlling network traffic, making them prime targets for attackers.

One fundamental practice in strengthening network device security is keeping these devices' firmware and software up to date. Manufacturers often release patches and updates to address security vulnerabilities and improve device performance.

To update network device firmware, administrators should access the device's web interface or command-line interface (CLI) and follow the manufacturer's instructions for applying updates.

For example, updating the firmware on a Cisco router involves the following CLI commands:

shell

enable   configure   terminal   boot   system flash:<new_firmware_filename> end write memory reload

In these commands:

enable enters privileged EXEC mode.

configure terminal enters global configuration mode.

boot system flash:<new_firmware_filename> specifies the new firmware file to be used.

end exits global configuration mode.

write memory saves the configuration.

reload restarts the router with the new firmware.

Regularly updating network device firmware is crucial in mitigating known vulnerabilities and enhancing security.

Another important practice is securing access to network devices by configuring strong authentication and authorization mechanisms. This includes setting strong passwords, employing multi-factor authentication (MFA), and implementing role-based access control (RBAC).

For example, configuring a Cisco router with strong password security involves:

shell

enable configure terminal enable secret <strong_password> line console 0 password <strong_password> login line vty 0 4 password <strong_password> login exit username <username> privilege 15 secret <strong_password> end write memory

In these commands:

enable secret <strong_password> sets a strong password for privileged EXEC mode.

line console 0 enters configuration mode for the console port.

password <strong_password> sets a strong password for console access.

login enables password-based login for the console.

line vty 0 4 enters configuration mode for virtual terminal lines.

password <strong_password> sets a strong password for remote access.

login enables password-based login for remote access.

exit exits line configuration mode.

username   <username>   privilege   15   secret <strong_password> creates a user account with full privileges.

end exits configuration mode.

write memory saves the configuration.

Implementing strong authentication and authorization measures ensures that only authorized personnel can access and configure network devices.

Additionally, network administrators should practice the principle of least privilege (PoLP) when configuring access controls. This means granting users and devices only the minimum level of access required to perform their tasks.

By adhering to the PoLP, administrators reduce the attack surface and limit the potential damage that can occur if unauthorized access or a breach occurs.

Network device security can also be enhanced by enabling and configuring intrusion detection and prevention systems (IDPS). These systems monitor network traffic for suspicious or malicious activities and can take action to block or mitigate threats.

For example, Cisco devices support the implementation of intrusion prevention through the use of access control lists (ACLs) and security policies. Administrators can configure ACLs to permit or deny specific traffic based on defined criteria.

To configure an ACL on a Cisco router, you can use the following commands:

shell

enable configure terminal access-list 101 deny tcp any host <protected_device_ip> eq 22 access-list 101 permit ip any any interface GigabitEthernet0/0 ip access-group 101 in end write memory

In these commands:

access-list 101 deny tcp any host <protected_device_ip> eq 22 denies incoming SSH traffic to the specified device.

access-list 101 permit ip any any allows all other traffic.

interface GigabitEthernet0/0 enters the configuration mode for the specified interface.

ip access-group 101 in applies the access list to incoming traffic on the interface.

end exits configuration mode.

write memory saves the configuration.

Configuring ACLs and security policies on network devices can help prevent unauthorized access and protect against specific threats.

Additionally, network administrators should regularly review and audit access controls, configurations, and security policies on network devices. Periodic security assessments help identify misconfigurations, weaknesses, or unauthorized changes that may have occurred over time.

Auditing network device configurations can be performed manually, but automated tools like NMAP can also be utilized to scan and assess network security. NMAP's scriptable scanning engine, NSE, allows administrators to develop custom scripts for specific security checks.

For example, a custom NMAP script can be created to scan a network for open ports and services on network devices and compare the findings to an expected baseline.

Automated audits can be scheduled to run regularly and generate reports that highlight any deviations or security concerns.

In summary, strengthening network device security is essential for safeguarding the integrity and availability of network infrastructure. This involves keeping firmware up to date, implementing strong authentication and authorization measures, following the principle of least privilege, enabling intrusion detection and prevention systems, configuring access controls, and conducting regular security audits. By taking these steps, organizations can significantly enhance their network device security posture and reduce the risk of intrusions and security breaches.

Device hardening is a crucial component of any organization's cybersecurity strategy. It involves implementing security measures and configurations to minimize vulnerabilities and protect network devices from potential threats.

One fundamental device hardening strategy is to change default passwords. Many network devices come with default usernames and passwords that are well-known to attackers.

To change the default password on a Cisco router, administrators can use the following CLI commands:

shell

enable configure terminal line console 0 password <new_password> login line vty 0 4 password <new_password> login end write memory

In these commands:

enable enters privileged EXEC mode.

configure terminal enters global configuration mode.

line console 0 enters configuration mode for the console port.

password <new_password> sets a new password for console access.

login enables password-based login for the console.

line vty 0 4 enters configuration mode for virtual terminal lines.

password <new_password> sets a new password for remote access.

login enables password-based login for remote access.

end exits configuration mode.

write memory saves the configuration.

Changing default passwords helps prevent unauthorized access and protects devices from common attacks.

Another critical aspect of device hardening is disabling unnecessary services and ports. Network devices often come with a wide range of services and ports enabled by default, some of which may not be required for the device's intended function.

Administrators should review the device's configuration and disable any services or ports that are not necessary for its operation. For example, if a Cisco switch does not need to run the Telnet service, it can be disabled using the following CLI commands:

shell

```
enable configure terminal no service telnet end write
memory
```

In these commands:

enable enters privileged EXEC mode.

configure terminal enters global configuration mode.

no service telnet disables the Telnet service.

end exits configuration mode.

write memory saves the configuration.

Disabling unnecessary services and ports reduces the attack surface and minimizes the risk of exploitation.

Additionally, implementing access control lists (ACLs) is a crucial device hardening strategy. ACLs can be used to control and restrict the flow of traffic to and from a network device.

For instance, on a Cisco router, administrators can configure an ACL to permit only specific IP addresses to access the device's management interface.

Here's an example of how to configure an ACL to restrict management access on a Cisco router:

shell

enable configure terminal access-list 100 permit ip <allowed_ip> <subnet_mask> access-list 100 deny ip any any line vty 0 4 access-class 100 in end write memory

In these commands:

enable enters privileged EXEC mode.

configure terminal enters global configuration mode.

access-list 100 permit ip <allowed_ip> <subnet_mask> permits traffic from the specified IP address and subnet.

access-list 100 deny ip any any denies all other traffic.

line vty 0 4 enters configuration mode for virtual terminal lines.

access-class 100 in applies the access list to incoming traffic on the virtual terminal lines.

end exits configuration mode.

write memory saves the configuration.

Implementing ACLs enhances device security by controlling who can access the device and what traffic is allowed.

Another critical device hardening practice is to regularly update the device's firmware and software. Manufacturers release updates and patches to address security vulnerabilities and improve device performance.

To update the firmware on a Cisco switch, administrators can use the following CLI commands:

shell

enable configure terminal archive download-sw /overwrite /reload tftp://<tftp_server_ip>/<firmware_filename>

In these commands:

enable enters privileged EXEC mode.

configure terminal enters global configuration mode.

archive download-sw /overwrite /reload tftp://<tftp_server_ip>/<firmware_filename> initiates a firmware download from a TFTP server, overwriting the existing firmware, and reloading the device.

Regularly updating firmware helps protect devices from known vulnerabilities and enhances their security.

Furthermore, device hardening involves implementing intrusion detection and prevention systems (IDPS) to monitor and protect against threats.

For example, organizations can deploy an IDPS like Snort to detect and prevent network-based attacks.

To install Snort on a Linux-based system, administrators can use the following CLI commands:

shell

sudo apt-get update sudo apt-get install snort

These commands update the package repository and install Snort on the system.

After installation, Snort can be configured to monitor network traffic, analyze packets, and trigger alerts or actions in response to suspicious activities.

Incorporating IDPS into device hardening measures provides an additional layer of security against network threats.

Lastly, device hardening should include the regular review and audit of device configurations and security policies.

Auditing can help identify misconfigurations, vulnerabilities, or unauthorized changes that may have occurred over time.

Automated tools and scripts can be used to scan and assess network device configurations.

For example, NMAP can be employed to scan network devices for open ports and services and compare the findings to an expected baseline.

Automated audits can be scheduled to run regularly and generate reports that highlight any deviations or security concerns.

In summary, device hardening is a critical practice in maintaining network security. Key strategies include changing default passwords, disabling unnecessary services and ports, implementing access control lists, updating firmware, deploying intrusion detection and prevention systems, and conducting regular security audits. By following these measures, organizations can strengthen the security of their network devices and reduce the risk of security breaches and vulnerabilities.

Chapter 7: Advanced NMAP Scanning for Defense

Proactive scanning for security is a critical practice in modern network defense strategies. In today's cybersecurity landscape, where threats are constantly evolving, organizations must take a proactive approach to identify vulnerabilities and security weaknesses before malicious actors can exploit them.

One fundamental aspect of proactive scanning is the regular assessment of network assets. Networks are dynamic, with devices and services constantly being added, removed, or modified.

To maintain an accurate understanding of the network's security posture, organizations should conduct regular scans to identify all devices and services that are currently active. Tools like NMAP can be used to perform these scans, providing insights into the network's current state.

For instance, administrators can use NMAP to scan a range of IP addresses to discover all active hosts on the network. The following CLI command can be used to conduct an IP address scan:

shell

nmap -sn 192.168.1.0/24

In this command:

nmap is the command to launch the NMAP tool.

-sn specifies a ping scan to discover active hosts without performing a full port scan.

192.168.1.0/24 represents the IP address range to be scanned.

Regular IP address scans help organizations maintain an up-to-date inventory of network assets.

Another essential aspect of proactive scanning is vulnerability assessment. Vulnerability scanning tools like Nessus or OpenVAS can be employed to identify known vulnerabilities in network devices, operating systems, and software applications.

For example, Nessus can be used to scan a network for common vulnerabilities by executing the following steps:

Launch Nessus and configure a new scan.

Define the target IP address range to scan.

Select the desired scan template, such as a "Full Scan."

Start the scan and analyze the results.

Nessus will provide a report detailing vulnerabilities found in the scanned network.

Additionally, organizations should conduct configuration audits on network devices to ensure they adhere to security best practices. These audits involve checking device configurations against established security baselines or compliance standards.

Tools like NMAP can be used to assess the security of network devices by comparing their configurations to predefined standards. Administrators can create custom NMAP scripts to perform these audits.

Regular configuration audits help organizations identify and rectify misconfigurations that could lead to security vulnerabilities.

Furthermore, organizations should implement continuous monitoring solutions that can detect and alert on suspicious or anomalous network activities. Intrusion detection systems (IDS) and security information and event management (SIEM) platforms are examples of such solutions.

IDS systems can analyze network traffic and raise alerts when they detect potentially malicious activities, such as unusual patterns or known attack signatures. SIEM platforms collect and correlate log data from various sources to identify security incidents.

To deploy an IDS system like Snort, administrators can follow these steps:

Install Snort on a dedicated server or appliance.

Configure Snort rules to detect specific threats or patterns.

Define alerting thresholds and actions.

Monitor the alerts generated by Snort and investigate suspicious activities.

SIEM platforms, on the other hand, require careful planning and integration with existing network infrastructure. Administrators should configure data sources, define correlation rules, and set up alerting mechanisms.

By deploying continuous monitoring solutions, organizations can detect and respond to security incidents in real-time, enhancing their proactive security posture.

Moreover, organizations should engage in penetration testing or ethical hacking to assess their network's resilience to real-world attacks. Penetration testers, often referred to as "ethical hackers," simulate attacks on the network to identify vulnerabilities and weaknesses.

Tools like NMAP can be utilized in penetration testing to gather information about the network, discover open ports, and identify potential attack vectors.

To perform a basic port scan during penetration testing, an ethical hacker may use a command like this:

shell

nmap -p 1-65535 <target_ip>

In this command:

-p 1-65535 specifies a full port scan, checking all ports from 1 to 65535.

<target_ip> represents the IP address of the target system.

Penetration testing should be conducted by skilled professionals who follow ethical guidelines and work within legal boundaries.

Furthermore, organizations should establish a vulnerability management program that includes processes for tracking, prioritizing, and remediating identified vulnerabilities. This program ensures that vulnerabilities are addressed in a systematic and timely manner.

To create a vulnerability management program, organizations can follow these steps:

Identify assets and their value to the organization.

Continuously scan and assess vulnerabilities.

Prioritize vulnerabilities based on severity and impact.

Develop remediation plans and timelines.

Implement patches, configuration changes, or mitigations.

Validate the effectiveness of remediation efforts.

By implementing proactive scanning for security, organizations can stay one step ahead of cyber threats, reduce their attack surface, and strengthen their overall cybersecurity posture.

In summary, proactive scanning is an essential practice in modern cybersecurity. It involves regular assessments of network assets, vulnerability scanning, configuration audits, continuous monitoring, penetration testing, and a structured vulnerability management program. By adopting these proactive measures, organizations can better defend against evolving cyber threats and minimize their exposure to potential security risks.

NMAP, known primarily as a network scanning and reconnaissance tool, can also be a valuable asset in enhancing network defense strategies. While it is true that NMAP is often associated with discovering vulnerabilities and weaknesses in networks, it can equally serve as a defense tool when used thoughtfully and strategically.

One of the essential defensive applications of NMAP is network mapping and asset discovery. By conducting regular network scans with NMAP, organizations can maintain an up-to-date inventory of all devices and services within their network. This comprehensive visibility is crucial for identifying unauthorized or rogue devices that may pose security risks.

For instance, a simple NMAP command like the following can be used to discover all active hosts on a network:

shell

nmap -sn 192.168.1.0/24

In this command, the **-sn** flag instructs NMAP to perform a ping scan, which identifies active hosts without conducting a full port scan. This information can be instrumental in recognizing any unexpected or unauthorized devices on the network.

Another defensive application of NMAP is the detection of open ports and services. While this capability is often associated with offensive security, it can be used defensively to ensure that only necessary ports and services are exposed.

NMAP can be employed to scan a network and list all open ports on each host. This information can then be compared against an organization's security policies to verify compliance and identify potential misconfigurations.

To perform a port scan with NMAP, an administrator can use a command like this:

shell

nmap -p 1-65535 <target_ip>

In this command, the **-p 1-65535** flag specifies a full port scan, checking all ports from 1 to 65535. The **<target_ip>** represents the IP address of the target system.

By regularly scanning for open ports and services, organizations can promptly identify any deviations from their security policies and take corrective actions.

Moreover, NMAP's scripting engine, known as the NSE (NMAP Scripting Engine), can be harnessed defensively. The NSE allows users to create custom scripts that automate various network-related tasks.

Defensively, organizations can develop NSE scripts to monitor network traffic for specific patterns or anomalies. For example, a custom NSE script can be created to detect and alert on unusual network traffic, such as repeated failed login attempts or unexpected data transfers.

The NSE script can run continuously and provide real-time alerts when suspicious activities are detected, aiding in the early detection of potential security incidents.

To illustrate the concept, here's a simplified example of an NSE script that monitors SSH login attempts and alerts if multiple failed login attempts occur within a short time frame:

```lua
local target_host = stdnse.get_script_args("target") local
last_login_attempt = {} local threshold = 3 local interval =
60 local function ssh_login_failed(host, port) local now =
os.time() if not last_login_attempt[host] then
last_login_attempt[host] = {} end if not
last_login_attempt[host][port] then
last_login_attempt[host][port] = now return false end
local time_since_last_attempt = now -
last_login_attempt[host][port]
```

last_login_attempt[host][port] = now if time_since_last_attempt < interval then return true end return false end action = function(host, port) if port.number == 22 and ssh_login_failed(host.ip, port.number) then return stdnse.format_output(true, "Multiple failed SSH login attempts detected on %s:%d", host.ip, port.number) end return stdnse.format_output(false, "No security concerns found on %s:%d", host.ip, port.number) end

In this simplified example, the NSE script monitors SSH login attempts and raises an alert if multiple failed attempts occur within a specified time interval.

By developing custom NSE scripts tailored to an organization's security requirements, defensive monitoring and alerting capabilities can be significantly enhanced.

Another defensive use of NMAP is the assessment of firewall and access control list (ACL) effectiveness. Organizations can employ NMAP to test whether their network defenses are configured correctly and to identify any potential weaknesses.

For example, an administrator can use NMAP to simulate an external scan and check which ports and services are accessible from the internet. This scan helps assess whether firewall rules and ACLs are appropriately blocking or allowing traffic.

To simulate an external scan with NMAP, a command like the following can be used:

shell

```
nmap -Pn -p 1-65535 -T4 -A <target_ip>
```

In this command, the **-Pn** flag disables host discovery (ping) to simulate an external perspective. The **-p 1-65535** flag specifies a full port scan, checking all ports from 1 to 65535.

The **-T4** flag sets the timing template for faster scanning, and the **-A** flag enables OS and service version detection.

By conducting such scans, organizations can verify that their firewall rules and ACLs effectively protect their network perimeter.

Furthermore, NMAP can be used defensively for intrusion detection and prevention. NMAP has the capability to detect and report changes in the network environment, such as the sudden appearance of new hosts or services.

Regularly scheduled NMAP scans can be configured to compare current scan results with historical data. Any discrepancies, such as new hosts or services, can trigger alerts, indicating potential security incidents or unauthorized changes.

Intrusion detection systems (IDS) can be integrated with NMAP to automate this process. NMAP scans can trigger IDS alerts, enabling immediate responses to network changes that may indicate security threats.

Lastly, NMAP can be employed defensively for network forensics and incident response. When a security incident occurs, NMAP can be used to gather detailed information about the affected systems, including open ports, running services, and potential vulnerabilities.

This information is invaluable for incident responders and forensic analysts in understanding the scope and impact of a security breach.

For example, after detecting a suspected compromise, an incident response team can use NMAP to conduct an in-depth scan of the affected host to identify any malicious activities or vulnerabilities that may have been exploited.

In summary, NMAP, often recognized for its offensive capabilities, can be a powerful defensive tool when used proactively and strategically. Organizations can leverage NMAP for network mapping, asset discovery, port scanning, custom NSE scripting for monitoring, firewall and ACL assessments, intrusion detection, and network forensics. By harnessing NMAP's defensive potential, organizations can bolster their network security and respond more effectively to emerging threats and incidents.

Chapter 8: Security Auditing and Compliance

Conducting security audits with NMAP is a fundamental practice in ensuring the robustness and resilience of an organization's network defenses. Security audits serve as a systematic examination of an organization's security infrastructure, policies, and configurations to identify vulnerabilities, weaknesses, and areas for improvement.

One of the primary objectives of a security audit is to evaluate the effectiveness of security controls and measures in place. NMAP, as a versatile and powerful network scanning tool, can play a pivotal role in this process.

An essential aspect of security audits with NMAP is the assessment of network devices, including routers, switches, firewalls, and intrusion detection systems (IDS). These devices are crucial components of an organization's security posture, and any misconfigurations or vulnerabilities can have significant repercussions.

NMAP can be used to scan these devices and identify potential weaknesses in their configurations. For example, an administrator can perform a firewall assessment by scanning the firewall's external interface to check for open ports that should not be accessible from the internet.

The following NMAP command illustrates how to scan a firewall's external interface:

shell

```
nmap -Pn -p 1-65535 -T4 -A <firewall_external_ip>
```

In this command, the **-Pn** flag disables host discovery (ping), the **-p 1-65535** flag specifies a full port scan, the **-T4** flag sets the timing template for faster scanning, and the **-A** flag enables OS and service version detection.

By conducting such scans on critical security devices, organizations can identify misconfigurations or unintended exposures that may need immediate attention.

Another crucial aspect of security audits is the examination of network services and applications. Organizations rely on various services to operate, and these services can be potential entry points for attackers.

NMAP can be used to scan and assess the security of these services, ensuring that they are appropriately configured and hardened. For instance, administrators can scan web servers to identify open ports and assess the security of web applications hosted on them.

Here's an example NMAP command for scanning a web server:

shell

```
nmap -p 80,443 -script http-enum <web_server_ip>
```

In this command, the **-p 80,443** flag specifies scanning ports 80 (HTTP) and 443 (HTTPS), and the **http-enum** script is used to enumerate information about the web server and hosted web applications.

By analyzing the results of such scans, organizations can detect vulnerabilities or misconfigurations in their web services and applications, allowing for timely remediation.

Security audits also encompass the examination of network architecture and topology. NMAP can be employed to map and visualize network topologies, providing insights into the overall network design and potential security risks.

The network mapping capabilities of NMAP allow administrators to discover the relationships between network devices, identify potential single points of failure, and assess network segmentation and isolation.

For example, the following NMAP command can be used to perform a network topology discovery scan:

shell

nmap -sn -T4 -oA topology_scan <network_subnet>

In this command, the **-sn** flag specifies a ping scan to discover active hosts without performing a full port scan. The **-T4** flag sets the timing template for faster scanning, and the **-oA** flag specifies the output format for the scan results.

By regularly mapping network topologies with NMAP, organizations can maintain a clear understanding of their network's layout and identify any unexpected or unauthorized devices connected to it.

Moreover, NMAP can be used to assess the security of wireless networks, including Wi-Fi access points and the devices connected to them. Security audits of wireless networks are essential to prevent unauthorized access and potential breaches.

Administrators can employ NMAP to conduct wireless scans, identify open Wi-Fi networks, and assess the security of the encryption and authentication methods used.

For example, the following NMAP command can be used to scan for open Wi-Fi networks:

shell

nmap -p 5353 --script=broadcast <wireless_network_subnet>

In this command, the **-p 5353** flag specifies scanning port 5353 (used by Apple's Bonjour service), and the **broadcast** script is used to identify open Wi-Fi networks.

By analyzing the results of these wireless scans, organizations can take steps to secure their wireless networks and mitigate the risk of unauthorized access.

Another critical aspect of security audits with NMAP is the identification of vulnerable services and outdated software. NMAP can be configured to scan for specific vulnerabilities and report on the software versions detected.

Organizations can use NMAP's vulnerability scanning capabilities to identify known vulnerabilities in the software and services running on their network devices.

For example, the following NMAP command can be used to scan for vulnerabilities in a specific service, such as an HTTP server:

shell

```
nmap -p 80 --script http-vuln-cve2020-27960 <web_server_ip>
```

In this command, the **-p 80** flag specifies scanning port 80 (HTTP), and the **http-vuln-cve2020-27960** script is used to check for a specific vulnerability (CVE-2020-27960) in the HTTP service.

By regularly scanning for vulnerabilities in this manner, organizations can stay informed about potential security risks and apply patches or mitigations as needed.

Furthermore, NMAP can assist in conducting compliance audits. Organizations may have specific security standards or regulatory requirements that they must adhere to.

NMAP can be configured to perform scans that check for compliance with these standards and generate reports that highlight areas of non-compliance.

For example, an organization subject to the Payment Card Industry Data Security Standard (PCI DSS) can use NMAP to scan for compliance with PCI DSS requirements.

By employing NMAP in compliance audits, organizations can ensure that they meet the necessary security standards and regulations.

In summary, conducting security audits with NMAP is an integral part of maintaining a robust and secure network environment. NMAP's capabilities in assessing security devices, services, network architecture, wireless networks, vulnerable software, and compliance standards make it a valuable tool for identifying security weaknesses and vulnerabilities. By regularly incorporating NMAP into their security audit processes, organizations can proactively strengthen their defenses and mitigate potential threats.

Ensuring regulatory compliance is a critical aspect of network security and governance, especially for organizations operating in highly regulated industries such as finance, healthcare, and government.
Compliance refers to adhering to specific laws, regulations, and industry standards that govern data security, privacy, and information management practices.
Failing to meet these compliance requirements can result in severe consequences, including fines, legal liabilities, damage to reputation, and potential data breaches.
NMAP can be a valuable tool in helping organizations ensure regulatory compliance by providing the means to conduct comprehensive security assessments and audits.
For example, organizations subject to the General Data Protection Regulation (GDPR) can utilize NMAP to assess the security of their networks and data handling processes to ensure compliance with GDPR's data protection requirements.
NMAP can be configured to scan for personal data leaks, unauthorized access points, or weak encryption methods that might put sensitive information at risk.
By regularly conducting these scans, organizations can identify and rectify compliance gaps before they lead to regulatory violations.
Furthermore, NMAP can be employed to assist organizations in complying with industry-specific regulations.
For instance, financial institutions often have to adhere to the Payment Card Industry Data Security Standard (PCI DSS) to protect customer payment card information.

NMAP can be used to scan for vulnerabilities in the network infrastructure, such as open ports or unpatched systems, that could potentially compromise payment card data.

By identifying and addressing these vulnerabilities proactively, organizations can maintain PCI DSS compliance and safeguard customer financial data.

Moreover, in the healthcare sector, organizations must adhere to the Health Insurance Portability and Accountability Act (HIPAA) to protect patient health information.

NMAP can be utilized to assess the security of healthcare networks, including the encryption and access controls in place to safeguard patient data.

Scanning for potential weaknesses or unauthorized access points can help healthcare organizations maintain HIPAA compliance and avoid costly penalties.

Additionally, government agencies often need to comply with security regulations and frameworks, such as the Federal Information Security Management Act (FISMA) in the United States.

NMAP can play a crucial role in helping government organizations assess the security of their networks, detect vulnerabilities, and ensure compliance with FISMA requirements.

For example, NMAP scans can identify open ports or services that may need additional security measures to align with FISMA guidelines.

In summary, NMAP serves as a valuable tool for organizations striving to ensure regulatory compliance in their respective industries.

By regularly scanning their network environments and addressing security vulnerabilities and weaknesses, organizations can demonstrate their commitment to compliance and safeguard against the potential legal and financial consequences of non-compliance.

NMAP's flexibility and versatility make it well-suited to adapt to various regulatory frameworks, helping organizations maintain a strong security posture and protect sensitive data.

In addition to compliance with external regulations, organizations must also consider internal security policies and standards to ensure comprehensive security.

Internal security policies are tailored to an organization's specific needs and risks, and they often serve as a foundation for maintaining a secure network environment.

NMAP can assist organizations in evaluating and enforcing their internal security policies effectively.

For example, organizations may have internal policies that require regular vulnerability assessments and patch management.

NMAP can automate vulnerability scanning by conducting regular assessments of network devices and identifying security weaknesses.

By adhering to internal security policies through NMAP's automated scanning capabilities, organizations can enhance their security posture and mitigate potential risks.

Furthermore, organizations often implement specific security controls and configurations based on their industry, size, and unique requirements.

NMAP can be customized to evaluate these controls and ensure that they are correctly implemented and effective.

For example, an organization may have a policy that all remote access points must use strong encryption protocols and enforce multi-factor authentication.

NMAP can be used to scan remote access points and verify that these security controls are in place and properly configured.

By aligning NMAP scans with internal security policies, organizations can validate their adherence to these policies and make informed decisions about areas that may require improvements.

Another essential aspect of ensuring regulatory compliance is documentation and reporting.

Organizations must maintain detailed records of their security assessments and audit results to demonstrate their commitment to compliance and provide evidence in case of regulatory inquiries or audits.

NMAP offers reporting capabilities that allow organizations to generate comprehensive reports of their security scans and assessments.

These reports can include details about identified vulnerabilities, system configurations, and security controls in place.

By documenting the results of NMAP scans and security assessments, organizations can establish a robust audit trail and evidence of their compliance efforts.

This documentation can be invaluable in regulatory audits or when responding to compliance inquiries from governing bodies or customers.

Moreover, NMAP's reporting capabilities can assist organizations in prioritizing remediation efforts.

Identified vulnerabilities can be categorized and ranked based on their severity and potential impact on compliance.

Organizations can use this information to prioritize the mitigation of critical vulnerabilities and allocate resources effectively.

In summary, NMAP is a powerful tool that can help organizations ensure regulatory compliance by conducting comprehensive security assessments, aligning with internal security policies, and maintaining detailed documentation of their security efforts.

By leveraging NMAP's capabilities and flexibility, organizations can proactively address security vulnerabilities, reduce compliance risks, and demonstrate their commitment to protecting sensitive data and information assets.

Whether complying with external regulations or internal security policies, NMAP can be a valuable ally in achieving and maintaining a strong security posture in today's complex and evolving threat landscape.

Chapter 9: Incident Response and Forensics

Incident response is a critical component of cybersecurity, aimed at effectively managing and mitigating security incidents when they occur.

NMAP can be a valuable asset in incident response, helping organizations quickly assess the scope and impact of an incident, identify compromised systems, and take appropriate actions to contain and remediate the threat.

One of the primary uses of NMAP in incident response is network reconnaissance.

When an organization suspects a security breach or compromise, it's essential to understand the extent of the incident.

NMAP can be used to scan the network and identify all active hosts and open ports.

By conducting an initial NMAP scan, incident responders can create a baseline of the network's normal state, allowing them to spot anomalies and unauthorized devices.

For example, if NMAP scans reveal unexpected open ports or unfamiliar systems, it could indicate a potential breach or unauthorized access.

In such cases, incident responders can investigate further and take appropriate actions.

Furthermore, NMAP can assist in identifying potentially compromised systems within the network.

Malicious actors often establish backdoors or pivot through compromised systems to maintain access.

NMAP scans can uncover these hidden backdoors or unauthorized services running on compromised hosts.

By regularly conducting NMAP scans, incident responders can detect such anomalies and address them promptly.

In the event of a security incident, incident responders can leverage NMAP to conduct thorough vulnerability assessments.

By scanning potentially compromised systems, NMAP can identify vulnerabilities or misconfigurations that may have been exploited by attackers.

For example, NMAP can be configured to perform version detection on open ports, revealing software versions and potential vulnerabilities associated with the services running on those ports.

Incident responders can then prioritize patching or remediation efforts to close security gaps and prevent further exploitation.

In addition to identifying vulnerabilities, NMAP can help incident responders assess the impact of an incident on network services and resources.

By conducting port scans and service detection, NMAP can determine which services are still operational and which may have been disrupted or compromised.

This information is crucial for understanding the extent of the incident and prioritizing the restoration of critical services.

NMAP's scripting engine, known as the NMAP Scripting Engine (NSE), can also play a vital role in incident response.

NSE allows incident responders to run custom scripts to automate specific tasks during an incident investigation.

For example, incident responders can use NSE scripts to check for signs of compromise, such as the presence of known malware files or suspicious registry entries.

These scripts can automate time-consuming tasks, enabling incident responders to focus on more complex analysis and containment efforts.

In some cases, incident responders may need to investigate the presence of rogue wireless access points (APs) that could be used to gain unauthorized access to the network.

NMAP can be configured to perform wireless scanning and detect the presence of rogue APs.

By identifying unauthorized wireless devices, incident responders can take steps to mitigate the risk and prevent further unauthorized access.

Furthermore, NMAP can assist in network traffic analysis during incident response.

By capturing and analyzing network packets, incident responders can gain insights into network communication patterns, potential data exfiltration, and suspicious activities.

NMAP can be used in conjunction with packet capture tools like Wireshark to perform detailed traffic analysis.

For example, incident responders can use NMAP to perform a targeted scan of a specific IP address or range and then analyze the resulting traffic for signs of malicious activity.

When conducting incident response with NMAP, it's crucial to use the tool responsibly and consider the potential impact on the network.

Scanning a large network with aggressive scan options can generate significant traffic and may disrupt network services.

Therefore, incident responders should carefully select scan options and tailor them to the specific needs of the investigation.

For example, using the "-T4" option for a faster scan may be appropriate for a small network segment, but it may not be suitable for scanning a large corporate network.

Similarly, using the "--max-rtt-timeout" option to control the maximum round-trip time for probes can help prevent long delays in scanning.

In summary, NMAP is a valuable asset in incident response, helping organizations assess the scope of security incidents, identify compromised systems, and conduct vulnerability assessments.

By using NMAP strategically and responsibly, incident responders can streamline their investigations, detect anomalies, and take swift actions to contain and remediate security threats.

With its versatility and customization options, NMAP is a powerful tool for incident responders dealing with the dynamic and evolving landscape of cybersecurity incidents.

Network forensics is a crucial discipline in cybersecurity that involves the investigation and analysis of network traffic, logs, and activities to uncover evidence of security incidents or malicious activities.

NMAP, with its versatile scanning and network mapping capabilities, can be a valuable tool in the field of network forensics, helping forensic analysts gather critical information and reconstruct events.

One of the primary applications of NMAP in network forensics is network discovery.

When a security incident occurs, forensic analysts often start by understanding the network's layout and identifying all connected devices.

NMAP can be used to conduct network discovery scans, revealing active hosts, open ports, and service banners.

For example, running the following NMAP command can help identify active hosts on a network:

nmap -sn 192.168.1.0/24

This command performs a ping scan ("-sn") on the specified IP range and provides a list of responsive hosts.

By conducting network discovery scans, forensic analysts can create an initial map of the network's architecture, which serves as the foundation for further investigation.

Once the network's layout is established, forensic analysts can use NMAP for deeper reconnaissance.

NMAP's comprehensive scanning options allow analysts to gather detailed information about hosts, services, and vulnerabilities.

For instance, conducting a service version detection scan can reveal the software versions running on open ports, potentially identifying outdated or vulnerable software:

nmap -sV -p 80,443 192.168.1.100

In this example, NMAP is used to scan ports 80 and 443 on host 192.168.1.100, providing information about the web services running on those ports.

By analyzing service versions and banners, forensic analysts can identify potential targets for exploitation and assess the security posture of the network.

In network forensics, it's often essential to reconstruct the timeline of events leading up to a security incident.

NMAP can assist in this process by providing timestamped scan results.

For example, using the "-T4" option for a faster scan and specifying the "--stats-every" option can generate timestamped statistics during the scan:

nmap -T4 --stats-every 60s 192.168.1.0/24

This command performs a scan on the specified IP range, and statistics are updated every 60 seconds, providing a timeline of scan progress.

These timestamped scan results can help forensic analysts correlate network activities with other logs and events, aiding in the reconstruction of the incident's timeline.

Moreover, NMAP's scripting engine, the NMAP Scripting Engine (NSE), can be a valuable asset in network forensics.

NSE allows analysts to develop custom scripts to automate specific tasks during an investigation.

For example, forensic analysts can create NSE scripts to extract information from web applications, query DNS records, or retrieve banners from open services.

These scripts can help gather evidence and contextual information related to the incident.

In addition to network scanning, NMAP can assist in the analysis of captured network traffic.

Network forensics often involves the examination of packet captures to identify suspicious activities or malicious traffic.

NMAP can be used in conjunction with packet capture tools like Wireshark to filter and analyze network traffic.

For instance, analysts can use NMAP to filter traffic related to a specific IP address or port range, making it easier to focus on relevant packets:

```
nmap --packet-trace -p 80,443 192.168.1.100
```

This command captures and traces packets on ports 80 and 443 for host 192.168.1.100, providing insights into the network traffic associated with those ports.

Furthermore, NMAP can help forensic analysts identify rogue or unauthorized devices on the network.

By conducting regular scans and comparing the results to an inventory of authorized devices, analysts can detect anomalies.

For example, NMAP can be configured to scan for open SSH or RDP ports, helping identify unauthorized remote access points:

```
nmap -p 22,3389 192.168.1.0/24
```

This command scans ports 22 (SSH) and 3389 (RDP) on the specified IP range, allowing analysts to spot potentially unauthorized access points.

In summary, NMAP is a valuable tool in the field of network forensics, assisting forensic analysts in network discovery, reconnaissance, timeline reconstruction, and evidence gathering.

With its robust scanning options, timestamped results, scripting capabilities, and compatibility with packet capture tools, NMAP equips analysts with the means to uncover critical information and insights during investigations.

Whether used to identify compromised systems, analyze network traffic, or detect unauthorized devices, NMAP plays a significant role in the forensic analysis of security incidents.

Chapter 10: Case Studies in Network Security

In the ever-evolving landscape of cybersecurity, organizations face a myriad of real-world security challenges that demand constant vigilance and proactive measures to protect their digital assets.

One of the foremost challenges is the persistent threat of malware.

Malicious software, in its various forms, continues to pose a significant risk to organizations of all sizes.

To combat this threat, organizations must deploy robust antivirus and anti-malware solutions that can detect and mitigate malware infections.

Tools like Windows Defender or third-party antivirus software provide essential protection by scanning files and processes for known malware signatures.

Additionally, organizations should implement regular system and software updates to patch vulnerabilities that malware often exploits.

Another pressing concern in today's digital landscape is the proliferation of ransomware attacks.

These attacks involve encrypting an organization's data and demanding a ransom for the decryption key.

To mitigate the risk of falling victim to ransomware, organizations must employ robust backup and disaster recovery strategies.

Frequent data backups stored in offline or secure locations can ensure data recovery without paying a ransom.

Moreover, employee training and awareness programs are crucial to educate staff about the dangers of phishing emails and social engineering tactics used to deliver ransomware.

Cybersecurity professionals also grapple with the challenge of securing remote work environments.

The COVID-19 pandemic accelerated the adoption of remote work, leading to a surge in remote access and collaboration tools.

Organizations must establish secure remote access policies and deploy Virtual Private Networks (VPNs) to safeguard data transmitted over untrusted networks.

Multi-factor authentication (MFA) is an essential security measure to verify the identities of remote users and protect sensitive resources.

Furthermore, securing Internet of Things (IoT) devices is an increasingly critical challenge.

IoT devices, such as smart cameras and thermostats, are vulnerable to exploitation if not properly configured and updated.

Organizations must segment IoT devices from critical networks, apply firmware updates regularly, and change default credentials to reduce the risk of compromise.

Cloud security presents its unique set of challenges.

As organizations migrate data and services to cloud platforms like Amazon Web Services (AWS) or Microsoft Azure, they must ensure proper configuration and access controls.

Misconfigurations in the cloud can lead to data exposure, and organizations must conduct regular security assessments to identify and rectify vulnerabilities.

Furthermore, data privacy regulations like the General Data Protection Regulation (GDPR) and the California

Consumer Privacy Act (CCPA) require organizations to protect customer data rigorously.

Compliance with these regulations entails implementing data encryption, access controls, and data retention policies.

Additionally, organizations must be prepared to report data breaches promptly to regulatory authorities and affected individuals.

The challenge of managing insider threats cannot be overlooked.

Insider threats, whether unintentional or malicious, can result in data breaches and other security incidents.

Employee training, access controls, and user monitoring are vital to detect and mitigate insider threats.

Organizations can also employ user and entity behavior analytics (UEBA) tools to identify abnormal user activities.

Social engineering attacks remain a significant security concern.

Phishing, pretexting, and baiting are tactics used by attackers to manipulate individuals into divulging sensitive information.

Employees should undergo regular security awareness training to recognize and thwart social engineering attempts.

Additionally, email filtering solutions can help detect and block phishing emails before they reach the inbox.

The challenge of vulnerability management is ongoing.

As software and systems age, new vulnerabilities emerge, and organizations must promptly patch or mitigate these vulnerabilities to prevent exploitation.

Vulnerability scanning tools like Nessus or OpenVAS can assist organizations in identifying and prioritizing vulnerabilities for remediation.

Lastly, regulatory compliance continues to be a substantial challenge for organizations.

Compliance requirements can vary based on industry, location, and the types of data processed.

Organizations must allocate resources to ensure they meet regulatory obligations, which often include data protection, reporting, and auditing requirements.

In summary, the field of cybersecurity is marked by a multitude of real-world security challenges.

From the persistence of malware and ransomware to securing remote work environments, IoT devices, and cloud platforms, organizations must adopt a comprehensive and proactive approach to cybersecurity.

Addressing these challenges demands a combination of technical solutions, employee training, and adherence to regulatory requirements.

By staying informed, vigilant, and adaptable, organizations can enhance their cybersecurity posture and protect their valuable assets in the digital age.

Examining real-world network security cases provides valuable insights and lessons for individuals and organizations striving to enhance their cybersecurity posture.

One notable case involves the breach of Equifax, one of the largest credit reporting agencies in the United States.

In this case, attackers exploited a known vulnerability in the Apache Struts web framework, which Equifax had failed to patch promptly.

The lesson here is the critical importance of timely software patching and vulnerability management.

Organizations must prioritize and systematically address known vulnerabilities to prevent exploitation.

The Equifax breach also highlights the significance of network segmentation.

Had Equifax segmented its critical systems from the compromised network segment, the attackers might have been contained, limiting the extent of the breach.

Segmentation is a powerful strategy to minimize lateral movement in the event of a breach.

Another instructive case is the Target breach in 2013.

Attackers gained access to Target's network through a third-party HVAC vendor.

This incident underscores the importance of supply chain security.

Organizations must assess and monitor the security of third-party vendors and enforce strict access controls for external entities.

A robust vendor risk management program can help prevent similar incidents.

The Stuxnet worm is a remarkable case that highlights the potential for state-sponsored cyberattacks.

Stuxnet was designed to target and disrupt Iran's nuclear program, demonstrating the ability of highly sophisticated malware to infiltrate critical infrastructure.

This case emphasizes the need for advanced threat detection capabilities and international cooperation in countering cyber threats.

The NotPetya ransomware attack in 2017 wreaked havoc on organizations worldwide.

NotPetya initially targeted Ukraine but quickly spread globally.

The attack demonstrated the destructive potential of ransomware and the importance of regular backups and disaster recovery plans.

Organizations should maintain up-to-date backups and conduct frequent recovery exercises.

The case of the Marriott data breach in 2018 highlights the significance of data encryption.

Marriott failed to encrypt sensitive guest data, leading to a massive data breach.

Encrypting sensitive information, both at rest and in transit, is a fundamental security practice to safeguard data from unauthorized access.

The WannaCry ransomware attack in 2017 exploited a Windows vulnerability for which a patch had been available.

This case underscores the critical need for a robust patch management process.

Organizations should apply patches promptly, especially for critical vulnerabilities, to prevent exploitation.

The breach of the U.S. Office of Personnel Management (OPM) in 2015 exposed sensitive information of millions of government employees.

This case highlights the importance of continuous monitoring and intrusion detection.

Timely detection of anomalous activities can help organizations identify and respond to breaches before extensive damage occurs.

The case of the Mirai botnet in 2016 illustrated the vulnerability of IoT devices.

Mirai infected IoT devices to launch massive DDoS attacks.

Securing IoT devices requires regular firmware updates, strong authentication, and proper network segmentation.

The Equifax breach, Target breach, Stuxnet, NotPetya, Marriott data breach, WannaCry, OPM breach, and Mirai botnet case studies collectively emphasize the multifaceted nature of network security challenges.

Each case offers distinct lessons, ranging from vulnerability management, supply chain security, and threat detection to data encryption, patch management, and IoT security.

These lessons underscore the need for a holistic and proactive approach to network security.

Moreover, these real-world cases demonstrate that cybersecurity is an ongoing endeavor that demands continuous improvement, adaptability, and collaboration among organizations and cybersecurity professionals.

By studying these cases and applying the lessons learned, individuals and organizations can better protect themselves against evolving cyber threats and vulnerabilities.

BOOK 4
NMAP BEYOND BOUNDARIES
MASTERING COMPLEX NETWORK RECONNAISSANCE

ROB BOTWRIGHT

Chapter 1: Advanced Reconnaissance Techniques

Passive reconnaissance methods are a crucial component of any comprehensive network scanning and security strategy. Unlike active reconnaissance, which involves direct interaction with a target network, passive reconnaissance techniques gather information without actively probing or engaging the target.

Passive reconnaissance methods are stealthy and less likely to trigger security alerts or alarms.

One of the most fundamental passive reconnaissance techniques is DNS (Domain Name System) enumeration.

DNS enumeration involves querying DNS servers for information about a target domain or organization.

This can reveal valuable information such as subdomains, mail server configurations, and potentially sensitive hostnames.

The "nslookup" command is a simple and widely used tool for DNS enumeration.

For example, to query DNS information for a domain, you can use the following command:

nslookup example.com

This command will provide you with the DNS records associated with the domain, including the IP addresses of its servers.

Another passive reconnaissance technique is email harvesting.

Email addresses are valuable pieces of information for cyber attackers, as they can be used for phishing campaigns or targeted attacks.

To harvest email addresses passively, attackers may scour publicly available sources such as websites, social media profiles, and online forums.

For example, using a command-line tool like "theHarvester," you can perform passive email harvesting by specifying a target domain:

theharvester -d example .com -l 100 -b google

This command will search Google for email addresses associated with the target domain and retrieve up to 100 results.

Passive reconnaissance can also involve monitoring network traffic and analyzing publicly available data.

This includes analyzing network traffic captured through passive network monitoring tools like Wireshark or Bro.

By examining the patterns of network traffic and identifying exposed services, attackers can gain insights into a target network's architecture and potential vulnerabilities.

Another passive method is analyzing WHOIS information.

WHOIS databases contain registration information for domain names and IP addresses.

By querying WHOIS databases, you can obtain details about the owner of a domain, their contact information, and the domain's registration history.

To query a WHOIS database for a domain, you can use command-line tools like "whois" or online WHOIS lookup services.

For example, to query the WHOIS information for the domain example.com, you can use the following command:

whois example.com

This command will provide you with registration details for the domain.

Passive reconnaissance also extends to social media and open-source intelligence (OSINT) gathering.

Attackers can search for information about an organization, its employees, and its technologies on social media platforms, forums, and public databases.

This information can be leveraged to craft targeted attacks or gain a better understanding of the organization's security posture.

One passive reconnaissance technique that is often overlooked is the analysis of error messages and HTTP status codes.

When a web server encounters an error or serves a specific HTTP status code, it may reveal information about its configuration, underlying technologies, or potential vulnerabilities.

By analyzing error messages and HTTP responses, attackers can gather intelligence about a target web application.

To examine HTTP headers and status codes, you can use command-line tools like "curl" or browser developer tools.

For instance, using "curl" to retrieve HTTP headers from a website:

arduino

```
curl -I https://example.com
```

Passive reconnaissance is not limited to external sources of information.

Internal passive reconnaissance techniques can also be employed within an organization's network.

This may involve monitoring internal network traffic, analyzing internal DNS records, or scrutinizing publicly available internal documentation.

For instance, examining internal DNS records can provide insights into an organization's internal network structure and naming conventions.

Overall, passive reconnaissance methods are a valuable component of any network scanning and security strategy.

They allow organizations to gather information about potential threats and vulnerabilities without alerting attackers to their presence.

However, it's essential to recognize that passive reconnaissance techniques can also be used by defenders to proactively identify and address security weaknesses in their networks.

By understanding and leveraging passive reconnaissance, organizations can enhance their overall cybersecurity posture and better defend against potential threats.

Active reconnaissance strategies are a critical component of network scanning and security assessments.

Unlike passive reconnaissance, which involves gathering information passively and without direct interaction, active reconnaissance methods involve actively probing and engaging with the target network.

Active reconnaissance is essential for identifying vulnerabilities, discovering open ports and services, and assessing the security posture of a network.

One of the fundamental active reconnaissance techniques is port scanning.

Port scanning involves sending network packets to a target system to determine which ports are open and what services are running on those ports.

A widely used tool for port scanning is Nmap, which provides a comprehensive set of features for scanning and analyzing target networks.

To perform a basic TCP SYN scan with Nmap, you can use the following command:

```
nmap -sS target_ip
```

This command sends TCP SYN packets to the target's ports and analyzes the responses to determine open ports and services.

Another essential active reconnaissance technique is service enumeration.

Once open ports have been identified through port scanning, service enumeration involves identifying the specific services and their versions running on those open ports.

Nmap also provides options for service enumeration. You can use the following command to perform service enumeration:

```
nmap -sV target_ip
```

This command will not only identify open ports but also attempt to determine the service and version information associated with each open port.

Active reconnaissance can also involve vulnerability scanning.

Vulnerability scanning tools like Nessus or OpenVAS can be used to scan target systems for known vulnerabilities.

These tools compare the service and version information obtained through active reconnaissance with a database of known vulnerabilities to identify potential security issues.

For example, using Nessus, you can initiate a vulnerability scan by providing the target IP address or hostname.

The results of the scan will provide information about any identified vulnerabilities, along with recommendations for remediation.

Another active reconnaissance technique is banner grabbing. Banner grabbing involves connecting to open ports and analyzing the banner or banner-like responses from the services running on those ports.

This can provide valuable information about the service and version.

Banner grabbing can be done using tools like Telnet or Netcat.

For example, to perform banner grabbing on port 80 (HTTP), you can use the following Netcat command:

```
nc target_ip 80
```

This command establishes a connection to the HTTP service on the target and displays the banner response, which often includes information about the web server and its version.

Active reconnaissance can also extend to brute-force attacks.

Brute-force attacks involve attempting to gain unauthorized access to services or systems by systematically trying various username and password combinations.

Tools like Hydra or Medusa are commonly used for brute-force attacks.

For example, to perform a brute-force attack against an SSH server with Hydra, you can use the following command:
bash

```
hydra -l username -P /path/to/wordlist ssh://target_ip
```

This command specifies the target IP, a username, and a wordlist of passwords to attempt.

While active reconnaissance techniques are essential for identifying vulnerabilities and assessing the security posture of a network, they must be used responsibly and ethically.

Unauthorized and aggressive scanning can disrupt services, trigger security alerts, and even violate legal regulations.

It's crucial to obtain proper authorization before conducting active reconnaissance activities on a network.

Additionally, organizations should prioritize security measures to defend against active reconnaissance, such as intrusion detection systems (IDS), intrusion prevention systems (IPS), and proper access controls.

In summary, active reconnaissance strategies are a fundamental aspect of network scanning and security assessments.

These techniques, including port scanning, service enumeration, vulnerability scanning, banner grabbing, and brute-force attacks, provide critical insights into a target network's vulnerabilities and security posture.

However, responsible and ethical use of these techniques, along with proper authorization, is essential to avoid potential legal and operational consequences.

Organizations must also implement security measures to protect against active reconnaissance and ensure the ongoing security of their networks.

Chapter 2: Targeted Host and Service Enumeration

Specific host enumeration techniques are essential for gathering detailed information about individual hosts within a network.

These techniques provide valuable insights into a host's operating system, open ports, installed services, and potential vulnerabilities.

One of the primary host enumeration methods is operating system fingerprinting.

Operating system fingerprinting involves identifying the specific operating system running on a target host.

Nmap, a popular network scanning tool, offers OS detection capabilities that allow you to determine the operating system of a host.

To perform OS detection with Nmap, you can use the following command:

mathematica

```
nmap -O target_ip
```

This command sends probes to the target host and analyzes the responses to make an educated guess about the operating system in use.

Another crucial host enumeration technique is port scanning, which was mentioned earlier in the context of active reconnaissance.

Port scanning helps identify the open ports on a host, which can provide clues about the services and applications running on that host.

By scanning specific ports, you can gain insights into the host's functionality.

For instance, if port 80 is open, it indicates that the host likely serves web content.

Additionally, if port 22 is open, it suggests SSH access.

Nmap provides various scan types for port enumeration, such as SYN scan, TCP connect scan, and UDP scan, among others.

Each scan type has its advantages and can reveal different details about the target host.

Service enumeration is another essential technique for specific host enumeration.

After identifying open ports on a host, it's essential to determine the specific services and their versions running on those ports.

Nmap offers service detection capabilities that enable you to accomplish this.

You can use the following command for service enumeration with Nmap:

nmap -sV target_ip

This command sends probes to the open ports and tries to identify the services based on their responses.

Service enumeration is crucial for understanding the host's functionality and potential vulnerabilities associated with the services.

Banner grabbing is a related technique used in service enumeration.

It involves connecting to a specific service on an open port and capturing the banner or initial response provided by that service.

The banner often includes information about the service and its version.

You can use tools like Telnet or Netcat for banner grabbing.

For example, to grab the banner from an HTTP server on port 80, you can use Netcat:

nc target_ip 80

This command establishes a connection to the HTTP server and displays the banner response, which may reveal details about the web server software and version.

Host enumeration can also extend to vulnerability scanning.

Once you've identified the services and their versions on a host, you can use vulnerability scanning tools like Nessus or OpenVAS to search for known vulnerabilities associated with those services.

These tools compare the service and version information with a database of known vulnerabilities and provide detailed reports on any identified issues.

Brute-force attacks can also be part of host enumeration techniques.

In specific scenarios, you may attempt to gain unauthorized access to a host by systematically trying various username and password combinations.

Tools like Hydra or Medusa are commonly used for brute-force attacks.

It's important to note that brute-force attacks should only be conducted with proper authorization and in compliance with ethical guidelines and legal regulations.

In summary, specific host enumeration techniques are essential for gathering detailed information about individual hosts within a network.

These techniques include operating system fingerprinting, port scanning, service enumeration, banner grabbing, vulnerability scanning, and brute-force attacks.

By applying these techniques responsibly and ethically, security professionals can gain a better understanding of a target host's characteristics and vulnerabilities, enabling them to take appropriate measures to secure the network effectively.

Service enumeration is a critical component of vulnerability assessment, allowing security professionals to gather detailed information about the services and applications running on a target system.

This process is essential for identifying potential security weaknesses and vulnerabilities that could be exploited by malicious actors.

One of the primary goals of service enumeration is to discover open ports on the target system.

Open ports are network interfaces that are actively listening for incoming connections, and they are a crucial entry point for attackers.

Nmap, a widely-used network scanning tool, provides various scan types for port enumeration, including SYN scan, TCP connect scan, and UDP scan.

Each scan type has its strengths and weaknesses, and the choice of scan type depends on the specific assessment requirements and the level of stealthiness desired.

For example, a SYN scan is faster and stealthier than a TCP connect scan, making it suitable for initial reconnaissance.

To perform a SYN scan with Nmap, you can use the following command:

nmap -sS target_ip

This command sends TCP SYN packets to the target's ports and analyzes the responses to determine open ports.

Once open ports have been identified, the next step in service enumeration is to determine the services and their versions running on those ports.

This is crucial because the service and version information can help security professionals assess the potential vulnerabilities associated with each service.

Nmap provides service detection capabilities that can identify services based on their responses to specific probes.

You can perform service enumeration with Nmap using the following command:

nmap -sV target_ip

This command sends probes to the open ports and attempts to identify the services and versions associated with each port.

Service enumeration can reveal valuable information about the target system's functionality and potential vulnerabilities.

However, it's important to note that some services may intentionally mislead or obfuscate their banners to thwart service detection.

In such cases, additional manual analysis may be required to accurately identify the services.

Banner grabbing is another technique used in service enumeration.

It involves connecting to a specific service on an open port and capturing the banner or initial response provided by that service.

The banner often includes information about the service and its version.

Tools like Telnet or Netcat can be used for banner grabbing.

For example, to grab the banner from an FTP server on port 21 using Netcat, you can use the following command:

nc target_ip 21

This command establishes a connection to the FTP server and displays the banner response, which may reveal details about the FTP server software and version.

Vulnerability scanning is an integral part of service enumeration for vulnerability assessment.

Once the services and their versions have been identified, security professionals can use vulnerability scanning tools like Nessus or OpenVAS to search for known vulnerabilities associated with those services.

These tools maintain databases of known vulnerabilities and can correlate the service and version information with the vulnerabilities.

For example, using Nessus, you can initiate a vulnerability scan by providing the target IP address or hostname.

The results of the scan will provide detailed information about any identified vulnerabilities, along with recommendations for remediation.

It's important to note that vulnerability scanning should always be conducted with proper authorization and in compliance with ethical guidelines and legal regulations.

Additionally, organizations should regularly patch and update their systems to address known vulnerabilities and reduce their attack surface.

In summary, service enumeration is a crucial phase in the vulnerability assessment process, allowing security professionals to identify open ports, discover services and their versions, and search for known vulnerabilities.

Tools like Nmap, banner grabbing, and vulnerability scanning are essential components of this process, providing valuable insights into a target system's security posture and potential weaknesses.

By conducting service enumeration responsibly and ethically, organizations can take proactive measures to enhance their security and protect their systems from potential threats.

Chapter 3: Custom NMAP Scripting for Deep Analysis

Writing NSE (Nmap Scripting Engine) scripts is a powerful way to extend the capabilities of Nmap and perform advanced network analysis and assessment.

These scripts are written in the Lua programming language, making them versatile and customizable for specific tasks.

Creating custom NSE scripts allows security professionals to tailor Nmap to their specific needs, whether it's for in-depth network reconnaissance, vulnerability assessment, or specialized tasks.

To start writing NSE scripts, you need a basic understanding of Lua programming.

Lua is known for its simplicity and readability, making it accessible to both experienced developers and those new to scripting.

You can use any text editor to write Lua scripts, but an integrated development environment (IDE) designed for Lua can enhance the scripting experience.

One popular Lua IDE is ZeroBrane Studio, which provides syntax highlighting and debugging features.

Before diving into NSE script writing, it's crucial to understand the Nmap Scripting Engine's architecture and how it interacts with Nmap.

The NSE is a collection of scripts that are executed during an Nmap scan, allowing for various network tasks to be automated and extended.

These scripts can be categorized into different types, such as discovery, exploitation, and vulnerability detection.

Each script is designed to perform a specific function, and you can write custom scripts to fit your requirements.

To create a custom NSE script, you'll typically follow a specific structure.

You'll define the script's name, description, categories, and dependencies at the beginning of the script file.

These details help Nmap categorize and execute the script appropriately.

You can also specify the script's author and license information to provide proper attribution.

Next, you'll define the script's action using Lua code.

This is where you implement the logic and functionality of the script.

For example, you might write a custom script to check for the presence of a particular web application on a target server.

Your script would send HTTP requests and analyze the responses to determine if the application is present.

Incorporating error handling in your script is essential to ensure that it behaves predictably and gracefully handles unexpected situations.

Within your script, you can use Nmap's Lua libraries and functions to interact with the scan data, host information, and network services.

These libraries provide useful tools for extracting and manipulating data during the scan.

For example, you can access the list of open ports on a target host or retrieve information about the operating system.

When your custom script is complete, you can save it with a ".nse" file extension.

This file should be placed in the Nmap scripts directory, which is typically located in the "scripts" subdirectory of the Nmap installation directory.

Once your script is in the right location, you can use Nmap's "-sC" option to run all scripts in the "default" category during a scan.

Alternatively, you can use the "--script" option to specify individual scripts to execute.

For example, to run a custom NSE script called "custom-script.nse," you can use the following command:

```
nmap --script custom-script.nse target_ip
```

By running your custom NSE script during an Nmap scan, you can automate specific tasks and gather valuable information about the target network.

These scripts can be used for a wide range of purposes, including banner grabbing, service enumeration, vulnerability detection, and more.

To ensure the effectiveness and reliability of your custom scripts, it's important to thoroughly test them in various network environments and scenarios.

Additionally, consider sharing your scripts with the Nmap community, as they may be valuable to other security professionals.

In summary, writing custom NSE scripts for advanced analysis with Nmap is a valuable skill for security professionals.

These scripts allow for the automation of network tasks and the customization of Nmap's functionality to meet specific needs.

With a solid understanding of Lua programming and Nmap's Lua libraries, you can create powerful scripts to enhance your network reconnaissance, vulnerability assessment, and overall security analysis efforts.

Leveraging the Nmap Scripting Engine (NSE) for complex scenarios allows security professionals to conduct comprehensive network assessments and address specific challenges in a customized manner. NSE, a powerful scripting framework integrated with Nmap, extends the tool's capabilities beyond simple port scanning and service enumeration.

To harness the full potential of NSE for complex scenarios, it's essential to understand its versatility and the range of scripts available. NSE scripts are written in Lua, a lightweight and easy-to-learn scripting language. Lua's flexibility and readability make it an ideal choice for scripting tasks within Nmap.

When dealing with complex network environments, NSE can provide tailored solutions that cater to specific needs. For instance, organizations may have unique security requirements, compliance standards, or complex infrastructures that demand a more nuanced approach to network assessment.

One significant advantage of NSE is its ability to automate tasks and perform advanced analysis during a scan. This can save time and effort, especially in scenarios where manual assessment would be impractical due to the size or complexity of the network.

To illustrate the power of NSE in complex scenarios, consider the following example. Suppose you need to assess the security of a large enterprise network with multiple subnets and thousands of hosts. A straightforward port scan may reveal open ports and services, but it may not provide the level of detail needed for a comprehensive assessment.

In this case, you can leverage NSE to create custom scripts that focus on specific aspects of the assessment. For instance, you can develop NSE scripts to:

Enumerate all running web servers and check for known vulnerabilities.

```
nmap -p 80,443 --script http-vuln-cve2021-26855.nse
target_subnet
```
Identify vulnerable versions of network services and prioritize patching.

```
nmap -p 22,3389 --script vulners.nse target_subnet
```
Conduct a thorough inventory of hosts, their operating systems, and installed software.

```
nmap -p 1-65535 --script smb-os-discovery.nse
target_subnet
```
Assess the configuration of network devices, such as routers and switches, for security weaknesses.

```
nmap -p 23,161,22 --script cisco-torch.nse target_subnet
```
By tailoring your NSE scripts to these specific tasks, you can obtain a deeper understanding of the network's security posture and prioritize remediation efforts effectively.

Another complexity that NSE can address is the need for compliance auditing. Many organizations are subject to regulatory requirements that mandate regular security assessments and compliance checks. NSE scripts can be designed to scan for specific compliance-related configurations or vulnerabilities.

For example, you can create NSE scripts to:

Check for weak SSL/TLS configurations and assess compliance with encryption standards.

```
nmap -p 443 --script ssl-enum-ciphers.nse target_subnet
```
Audit web server configurations to ensure they adhere to security best practices.

```
nmap -p 80,443 --script http-security-headers.nse
target_subnet
```
Verify compliance with industry-specific standards, such as HIPAA or PCI DSS.

arduino

```
nmap --script=ssl-cert,ssl-enum-ciphers -p 443
target_subnet | grep "Subject:"
```

By automating compliance checks using NSE scripts, organizations can maintain a continuous and proactive approach to security and regulatory compliance.

Complex scenarios may also involve the assessment of diverse and distributed networks, including cloud-based assets and IoT devices. NSE can be adapted to handle such challenges by incorporating cloud-specific scripts and IoT-related checks.

For example, you can utilize NSE scripts to:

Assess the security of cloud-based assets and services.

```
nmap -p 80,443 --script=ssl-cert,ssl-enum-ciphers -iL
cloud_assets.txt
```

Conduct security assessments of IoT devices within a network.

```
nmap -p 80,443 --script iot-vuln-check.nse target_subnet
```

Evaluate the exposure of cloud storage buckets to potential data leaks.

```
nmap -p 80,443 --script s3-bucket.nse target_subnet
```

By incorporating cloud and IoT-specific NSE scripts into your assessments, you can ensure that no critical aspect of your network's security is left unexamined.

In summary, leveraging the Nmap Scripting Engine (NSE) for complex scenarios offers security professionals the flexibility and customization required to address unique challenges in network assessment and compliance auditing.

By creating custom NSE scripts tailored to specific tasks and requirements, organizations can automate assessments, conduct thorough security checks, and ensure compliance with regulatory standards.

NSE's adaptability makes it an indispensable tool for security professionals working in diverse and complex network environments, enabling them to stay ahead of emerging threats and vulnerabilities.

Chapter 4: Geospatial Network Mapping

Mapping networks with geographic data is a crucial aspect of network reconnaissance and security assessment in today's interconnected world. This technique combines the power of network mapping and geospatial visualization to gain a deeper understanding of the physical and logical layout of networks.

To effectively map networks with geographic data, professionals often employ tools and techniques that enable them to visualize the geographical distribution of network assets and connections. One such tool that plays a pivotal role in this process is Nmap, a versatile and widely used network scanning utility.

Using Nmap for geographic network mapping involves a series of steps that allow you to collect valuable information about network hosts and their geographical locations. The first step is to conduct a network scan to identify live hosts and open ports within the target network.

shell

nmap -sn target_subnet

The **-sn** option in the Nmap command stands for "ping scan," which is used to discover live hosts without performing a full port scan. This initial scan provides a list of active hosts, which forms the foundation of the geographic mapping process.

Once you have identified the live hosts, the next step is to gather additional information about them, such as their operating systems and open ports. This can be achieved by running a more comprehensive scan using Nmap's service detection capabilities.

shell

nmap -A target_subnet

The **-A** option instructs Nmap to perform an aggressive scan, which includes service detection, OS detection, and script scanning. This scan provides detailed information about each host, including the services they are running and their operating systems.

With the information collected from the network scan, you can now proceed to map the network geographically. There are several methods and tools available for this purpose, but one commonly used approach involves leveraging the host's IP addresses and geolocation databases.

There are online geolocation databases and APIs, such as MaxMind's GeoIP2, that can be used to determine the approximate geographical location of an IP address. These databases provide information about the country, city, and even latitude and longitude coordinates associated with an IP address.

You can integrate these geolocation databases with your Nmap scan results to map the discovered hosts to their respective geographic locations. This can be accomplished by writing custom scripts or using existing tools that automate the process.

For example, you can use a Python script to query a geolocation database and plot the IP addresses on a map. Here's a simplified example using Python and the MaxMind GeoIP2 Python library:

python

import geoip2.database import folium # Create a map object m = folium.Map(location=[0, 0], zoom_start=2) # Open the GeoIP database reader = geoip2.database.Reader('GeoLite2-City.mmdb') # List of IP addresses from Nmap scan ip_addresses = ['192.168.1.1', '203.0.113.1', '104.16.249.249'] # Replace with actual IP addresses # Iterate through IP addresses and add markers to the map for ip in ip_addresses: try: response = reader.city(ip) lat = response.location.latitude lon = response.location.longitude folium.Marker([lat, lon], tooltip=f'IP: {ip}').add_to(m) except geoip2.errors.AddressNotFoundError: pass # Save the map to an HTML file m.save('network_map.html')

In this example, the script uses the MaxMind GeoIP2 library to retrieve geographic information for each IP address and plots them as markers on a map using the Folium library. The resulting HTML file can be opened in a web browser to visualize the geographic distribution of network hosts.

Mapping networks with geographic data not only helps in understanding the physical layout of networks but also assists in identifying potential security risks and optimizing network infrastructure. By visualizing the geographical distribution of hosts and their connections, organizations can make informed decisions regarding network segmentation, disaster recovery planning, and resource allocation.

Moreover, this technique is valuable for identifying anomalies or unauthorized access from unexpected geographic locations, which can be indicative of security breaches or suspicious activities.

In summary, mapping networks with geographic data is a powerful technique that combines the capabilities of network scanning tools like Nmap with geolocation databases to provide insights into the physical and logical structure of networks. This approach aids in network visualization, security assessment, and informed decision-making for network administrators and security professionals.

Analyzing network topology in a geospatial context is a

sophisticated approach to understanding the intricate relationships between network components and their physical locations. This technique integrates traditional network topology mapping with geographic information systems (GIS) to provide a comprehensive view of network infrastructure.

One of the key advantages of analyzing network topology in a geospatial context is the ability to visualize how network elements are distributed across geographical areas. This visualization is particularly valuable for organizations with extensive and geographically dispersed networks, such as multinational corporations, government agencies, and large data centers.

To effectively analyze network topology in a geospatial context, professionals often rely on specialized tools and methodologies. Geographic information systems (GIS) software, such as ArcGIS or QGIS, are commonly used for this purpose. These tools allow network administrators and analysts to overlay network topology data onto geographical maps, creating a visual representation of the network's physical layout.

The process typically begins with the collection of network topology data, which includes information about routers, switches, servers, and other network devices. This data may be obtained through network discovery tools or network management systems that monitor and document the network's configuration.

Once the network topology data is collected, it can be imported into the GIS software. Network administrators can then create layers on the map to represent different types of network elements. For example, routers may be represented by one layer, switches by another, and servers by yet another.

Geospatial analysis tools within GIS software can help identify patterns and trends within the network's geographical layout. For instance, analysts can use proximity analysis to determine which network devices are physically close to each other, potentially indicating redundancy or vulnerability in network design.

Another valuable aspect of analyzing network topology in a geospatial context is the ability to assess network performance and optimize resource allocation. By overlaying network traffic data onto the geographical map, administrators can pinpoint areas of high network activity and allocate resources accordingly.

Moreover, this technique can aid in disaster recovery planning. By visualizing the geographical distribution of network components, organizations can identify critical nodes that may need redundancy or backup solutions in case of a network outage or natural disaster.

Security is also a significant concern in network topology analysis. GIS can be used to visualize network access points and potential security vulnerabilities. For example, identifying network elements located in high-risk geographical areas or those exposed to external threats can help organizations enhance their security measures.

Additionally, analyzing network topology in a geospatial context can assist in compliance with regulatory requirements. For industries with specific geographic constraints or regulations, such as telecommunications or utilities, this technique can ensure that network infrastructure complies with geographical regulations and standards.

To demonstrate the practical application of this technique, let's consider an example. Suppose a multinational corporation operates data centers in different regions around the world. Analyzing the network topology in a geospatial context can reveal which data centers are underutilized and which are experiencing high traffic loads. This information can guide decisions on load balancing, resource allocation, and potential data center consolidation.

In summary, analyzing network topology in a geospatial context is a powerful approach that combines GIS technology with network management to provide a holistic view of network infrastructure. This technique offers benefits in terms of visualization, optimization, disaster recovery planning, security assessment, and regulatory compliance. By leveraging geospatial analysis, organizations can make informed decisions about their network architecture and improve overall network efficiency and resilience.

Chapter 5: NMAP and IoT Security

IoT device discovery and assessment are critical aspects of modern network security, given the rapid proliferation of internet-connected devices. This chapter explores techniques and methodologies for identifying, categorizing, and assessing IoT devices within your network.

The Internet of Things (IoT) encompasses a vast array of devices, from smart thermostats and wearables to industrial sensors and connected appliances. These devices often have varying levels of security and can pose risks if not properly managed.

To begin the process of IoT device discovery, you need to employ network scanning tools and techniques. One commonly used tool for this purpose is Nmap, a versatile open-source network scanner. With Nmap, you can perform both basic and advanced scans to identify devices on your network.

A basic IoT device discovery scan with Nmap might involve the following command:

shell

nmap -sn 192.168.1.0/24

This command conducts a ping scan on a specific subnet, attempting to discover active devices. The **-sn** flag instructs Nmap to perform a simple host discovery without conducting port scans.

Once you've identified devices, it's crucial to classify them based on their function and purpose. IoT devices can fall into various categories, such as consumer IoT (smart home devices), industrial IoT (sensors and controllers), or healthcare IoT (medical devices).

Creating a comprehensive inventory of IoT devices is essential for network management and security. You can use tools like spreadsheets or dedicated asset management software to track and categorize these devices.

After creating an inventory, the next step is assessing the security of IoT devices. Many IoT devices have limited security features, making them potential targets for cyberattacks. Vulnerabilities can arise from weak passwords, outdated firmware, or insecure communication protocols.

One approach to assessing IoT device security is conducting vulnerability scans. Tools like Nessus or OpenVAS can help identify known vulnerabilities in IoT devices. These tools generate reports that highlight security weaknesses and provide recommendations for remediation.

To use Nessus for vulnerability assessment, you might execute the following command:

shell

nessus -q -T html -x -c scan_policy -r report.html

In this command, Nessus scans devices based on the configured policy (scan_policy) and generates an HTML report (report.html) with detailed findings.

In addition to vulnerability scans, it's essential to evaluate the network behavior of IoT devices. Tools like Wireshark allow you to capture and analyze network traffic generated by these devices.

To capture traffic from a specific IoT device using Wireshark, follow these steps:

Identify the IP address of the IoT device using Nmap or your network management software.

Start a packet capture session on the network interface where the IoT device is connected.

Apply a display filter to isolate traffic from the specific IP address. For example, if the IoT device's IP is 192.168.1.100, use the filter **ip.addr == 192.168.1.100**.

Analyze the captured traffic for anomalies or unexpected communication patterns.

By monitoring network traffic, you can identify potential security issues, such as unauthorized data transfers or unusual device behavior.

Another critical aspect of IoT device assessment is ensuring that devices are running up-to-date firmware and software. Outdated firmware can contain known vulnerabilities that attackers can exploit. Therefore, regularly checking for updates and applying patches is crucial.

In some cases, IoT devices may not support automatic updates, requiring manual intervention. This involves visiting the manufacturer's website, downloading the latest firmware, and following specific instructions to update the device.

Additionally, it's essential to assess the authentication and access control mechanisms of IoT devices. Weak or default credentials can make devices vulnerable to unauthorized access. Ensure that devices use strong, unique passwords and consider implementing two-factor authentication (2FA) wherever possible.

IoT devices often communicate using various protocols, including HTTP, MQTT, and CoAP. Understanding these protocols is vital for assessing device security. For example, devices using insecure communication protocols like HTTP may transmit sensitive data in plaintext, making it susceptible to interception.

To assess the security of IoT device communication, you can use network monitoring tools like Wireshark to capture and analyze network traffic. Look for instances of plaintext data transmission, unencrypted credentials, or unusual communication patterns.

Another aspect of IoT device assessment involves evaluating the physical security of the devices. Ensure that physical access to critical IoT devices is restricted to authorized personnel only. This prevents tampering or theft of devices, which could lead to security breaches.

Furthermore, consider implementing network segmentation to isolate IoT devices from critical network segments. This limits the potential impact of a compromised IoT device on the overall network security.

In summary, IoT device discovery and assessment are crucial for maintaining network security in an increasingly connected world. By employing network scanning tools like Nmap, conducting vulnerability assessments, monitoring network traffic, and evaluating device security practices, organizations can mitigate the risks associated with IoT devices. Regular updates, strong authentication, and physical security measures also play vital roles in safeguarding IoT ecosystems.

As the Internet of Things (IoT) continues to expand, the practice of scanning and assessing IoT devices on a network becomes increasingly critical. However, it's equally important to understand the security implications associated with IoT scanning, as this chapter will explore.

IoT scanning, which involves the identification and evaluation of IoT devices on a network, can expose several security considerations that organizations need to address. One of the primary concerns is the potential for unauthorized or malicious scanning activities.

When conducting IoT scans, organizations must ensure that the scanning process itself is secure. Scanning tools like Nmap can generate network traffic and send requests to IoT devices. If not properly configured, these scans could inadvertently disrupt device operations or trigger false alarms on intrusion detection systems (IDS).

To mitigate these risks, it's essential to use scanning tools responsibly and consider the potential impact on IoT devices. This includes scheduling scans during non-business hours to minimize disruption and using scan configurations that are less likely to trigger false positives.

Another security consideration is the privacy of data collected during IoT scanning. Scanning can reveal sensitive information about IoT devices, such as device names, manufacturers, and firmware versions. This information may be valuable to attackers seeking to exploit known vulnerabilities in specific device models.

To address privacy concerns, organizations should implement proper data handling and retention policies. Only collect and store the data necessary for network management and security. Additionally, ensure that any sensitive information obtained during scanning is adequately protected, and access to this data is restricted to authorized personnel.

IoT devices are notorious for their limited security features and the use of default or weak credentials. When scanning IoT devices, it's common to encounter devices with easily guessable usernames and passwords, which can pose significant security risks.

To address this issue, IoT scanning should be combined with credential testing to identify devices using weak or default credentials. Scanning tools like Nmap can integrate with credential testing modules to automate this process. For example, the Nmap NSE script "brute" can be used to test common usernames and passwords against IoT devices.

Here's an example of how to use the "brute" NSE script with Nmap:

shell

```
nmap -p 22 --script ssh-brute <target>
```

In this command, Nmap is instructed to perform a brute-force SSH login attempt on the specified target to test for weak SSH credentials.

Additionally, organizations should prioritize the practice of changing default passwords on IoT devices and implementing strong, unique credentials. Many IoT devices lack robust authentication mechanisms, making them vulnerable to unauthorized access.

Another security implication of IoT scanning is the potential exposure of device interfaces and services to the internet. Scanning can reveal open ports, services, and web interfaces that may not be intended for public access. Attackers often seek to exploit these exposed services to gain unauthorized control of IoT devices.

To address this concern, organizations should employ access control measures to restrict access to IoT device interfaces and services. This may involve firewall rules, virtual private networks (VPNs), or network segmentation to isolate IoT devices from the public internet.

Furthermore, organizations should regularly monitor and log access attempts to these interfaces and services to detect and respond to any unauthorized activity promptly.

In some cases, IoT scanning may inadvertently disrupt the operation of IoT devices, especially if the scanning process generates excessive traffic or sends unexpected requests. Organizations need to consider the potential impact on critical IoT devices and services when conducting scans.

To minimize disruption, it's essential to conduct scans during non-critical hours and adjust scan parameters to limit the scanning traffic. Additionally, organizations should have contingency plans in place to handle any unexpected disruptions caused by scanning activities.

Another security implication is the potential identification of unknown or unauthorized IoT devices on the network. While discovering previously unidentified devices can enhance network visibility, it can also raise concerns about unauthorized devices that may have been added without proper authorization.

To address this issue, organizations should implement strict device onboarding and registration procedures. All IoT devices should undergo a vetting process before being allowed on the network. This includes verifying the legitimacy of the device, checking for security vulnerabilities, and ensuring compliance with network policies.

Additionally, network administrators should regularly review the results of IoT scans to identify any devices that should not be on the network. Any unauthorized or rogue devices should be promptly investigated and removed.

In summary, IoT scanning is a crucial practice for maintaining the security and integrity of IoT ecosystems. However, organizations must be aware of the potential security implications associated with scanning activities. By following responsible scanning practices, implementing strong authentication measures, protecting sensitive data, and monitoring access to device interfaces, organizations can effectively address these security concerns and enhance the overall security posture of their IoT networks.

Chapter 6: Cloud Network Scanning

In today's interconnected world, where cloud computing has become the backbone of many organizations' IT infrastructure, the need to scan and assess the security of cloud environments is paramount. Cloud infrastructure scanning involves the identification and evaluation of assets, vulnerabilities, and potential threats within cloud-based systems and services.

As more businesses migrate their operations to cloud providers like Amazon Web Services (AWS), Microsoft Azure, and Google Cloud Platform (GCP), understanding how to conduct effective and secure cloud infrastructure scanning is essential. This chapter explores the techniques and considerations for scanning cloud environments.

One of the primary motivations for scanning cloud infrastructure is to ensure the security and compliance of cloud resources. Cloud providers offer a range of services and configurations, and it's crucial for organizations to have visibility into their cloud assets and their security posture.

To initiate a scan of cloud infrastructure, the first step is to identify the scope of the assessment. Organizations should specify the cloud regions, accounts, and resources they want to include in the scan. For example, if an organization uses multiple AWS accounts across different regions, they can define the scope accordingly.

Here's an example of how to initiate a scan using the AWS Command Line Interface (CLI):

shell

```
aws ec2 describe-instances --region us-east-1
```
In this command, the "describe-instances" operation is used to list the details of EC2 instances in the "us-east-1" region. This is a basic example, and more advanced scanning tools and techniques can be employed depending on the complexity of the cloud environment.

Scanning cloud infrastructure requires the use of specialized tools and methodologies designed to work within the cloud context. These tools are often capable of discovering and assessing various cloud services and resources, such as virtual machines, databases, storage buckets, and more.

Organizations can leverage cloud-native security tools and services provided by their cloud providers. For instance, AWS offers AWS Inspector and AWS Config for vulnerability assessment and configuration management. Similarly, Azure provides Azure Security Center, which includes threat detection and vulnerability assessment features.

In addition to cloud provider-specific tools, organizations can also utilize third-party security scanning solutions that are compatible with multiple cloud platforms. These tools offer comprehensive scanning capabilities and can provide a unified view of security across heterogeneous cloud environments.

As organizations scan their cloud infrastructure, they may encounter challenges related to the dynamic nature of cloud resources. Cloud environments are highly scalable and elastic, which means that resources can be provisioned, modified, or decommissioned rapidly. This dynamic nature requires continuous monitoring and scanning to keep up with changes.

Automation plays a vital role in addressing this challenge. Cloud security teams can implement automated scanning and assessment processes that trigger scans whenever changes are detected in the cloud environment. This ensures that new resources and configurations are promptly evaluated for security compliance.

Another critical aspect of cloud infrastructure scanning is the identification and assessment of misconfigurations. Misconfigurations are one of the leading causes of security breaches in the cloud. They can expose sensitive data, weaken access controls, and leave cloud resources vulnerable to attacks.

To detect misconfigurations, scanning tools examine cloud resource configurations against predefined security baselines and best practices. For example, a misconfiguration may involve an S3 bucket with public access enabled, which can lead to data exposure. Scanning tools can identify such misconfigurations and provide recommendations for remediation.

Here's an example of scanning for S3 bucket permissions using the AWS CLI:

shell

```
aws s3 ls s3:// --recursive --human-readable --summarize
```

This command lists all S3 buckets and their contents, allowing administrators to review permissions and configurations. Regularly conducting such scans can help identify and rectify misconfigurations.

Cloud infrastructure scanning also extends to network security. Organizations need to assess the security groups, firewalls, and network access controls within their cloud environment. This includes reviewing inbound and outbound traffic rules to ensure that only authorized communication is allowed.

Network scanning tools, such as Nmap and Nessus, can be adapted for cloud environments. By specifying the cloud region and security group associated with a resource, these tools can evaluate network access rules and identify potential vulnerabilities.

Here's an example of using Nmap to scan an AWS EC2 instance in a specific security group:

shell

```
nmap -p 1-65535 -sV -Pn -T4 -iL targets.txt
```

In this command, "targets.txt" would contain the list of EC2 instance IP addresses associated with the specified security group.

Scanning cloud infrastructure also involves assessing the compliance of cloud resources with industry regulations and organizational policies. Compliance requirements may vary based on the type of data and services hosted in the cloud.

Cloud providers often offer compliance certifications for their services, such as SOC 2, ISO 27001, or HIPAA. Organizations can use scanning tools to verify that their cloud resources adhere to these certifications and align with their compliance goals.

In summary, scanning cloud infrastructure is an integral part of ensuring the security, compliance, and resilience of modern IT environments. As organizations continue to embrace cloud computing, they must implement robust scanning practices and leverage the right tools and methodologies to assess their cloud resources effectively. By regularly scanning and monitoring cloud environments, organizations can proactively identify and address security risks, misconfigurations, and compliance gaps, ultimately strengthening their cloud security posture.

In the realm of cloud network scanning, there are several critical security considerations that organizations must address to ensure the safety and integrity of their cloud environments. As businesses increasingly rely on cloud services and infrastructure, it becomes paramount to conduct network scanning activities with a security-first mindset.

One of the primary security concerns in cloud network scanning is data privacy and confidentiality. Cloud environments often host sensitive information, and scanning activities may inadvertently expose this data if not carefully managed. To mitigate this risk, organizations should implement proper access controls and encryption mechanisms to safeguard data during scanning.

For example, when using scanning tools in the cloud, it's essential to restrict access to those tools to authorized personnel only. The use of role-based access control (RBAC) and multi-factor authentication (MFA) can help ensure that only trusted individuals can initiate and monitor scans.

Moreover, data transmitted during scanning should be encrypted to protect it from interception. When configuring scanning tools, organizations should enable secure communication protocols such as HTTPS or SSH to encrypt data in transit. This ensures that any data sent to or received from cloud resources remains confidential.

Another critical security consideration is the potential impact of scanning activities on cloud resources and services. Scanning can be resource-intensive and may consume significant CPU, memory, and network bandwidth. If not carefully managed, scanning activities can lead to service disruptions or performance degradation in a shared cloud environment.

To address this concern, organizations should schedule scanning activities during off-peak hours or use cloud provider-specific features like AWS Elastic Beanstalk to auto-scale resources as needed. Additionally, organizations can employ scanning tools that allow them to limit the scan intensity to prevent overloading cloud resources.

Security teams should also be mindful of the potential for false positives and false negatives during cloud network scanning. False positives occur when scanning tools incorrectly identify vulnerabilities or misconfigurations that do not exist, while false negatives occur when actual vulnerabilities go undetected.

To reduce false positives, organizations should regularly update their scanning tools and vulnerability databases to ensure they have the latest information. Additionally, fine-tuning scan parameters and using authentication where applicable can help improve the accuracy of scans.

To address false negatives, organizations should consider using multiple scanning tools and techniques to cross-verify results. Additionally, conducting manual reviews and penetration testing can help uncover vulnerabilities that automated scanning tools may miss.

Furthermore, organizations should be cautious about the impact of scanning on intrusion detection and prevention systems (IDS/IPS) in the cloud. Some scanning activities may trigger alerts in IDS/IPS solutions, potentially leading to false alarms or even automatic blockage of scanning traffic.

To mitigate this risk, organizations should coordinate with their cloud provider's security teams to whitelist scanning traffic and avoid triggering IDS/IPS alerts. It's crucial to maintain clear communication to ensure that security measures do not interfere with legitimate scanning activities.

Additionally, when conducting scans that involve port scanning or vulnerability assessment, organizations should use scanning tools and techniques that are specifically designed for cloud environments. Cloud-native scanning solutions are optimized for the unique challenges and dynamics of cloud networks.

As cloud environments are constantly evolving, with resources being provisioned and decommissioned on-demand, maintaining an accurate inventory of assets can be challenging. Security teams need to ensure that scanning activities cover all relevant cloud resources and accounts.

To achieve this, organizations should implement continuous monitoring and asset discovery mechanisms. Tools like AWS Config and Azure Resource Graph can help maintain an up-to-date inventory of cloud assets, making it easier to target scanning activities effectively.

Moreover, organizations should align their cloud network scanning efforts with industry best practices and compliance standards. Many regulations, such as the General Data Protection Regulation (GDPR) and the Health Insurance Portability and Accountability Act (HIPAA), require regular security assessments and vulnerability scanning.

By adhering to these standards, organizations not only enhance their security posture but also demonstrate their commitment to compliance and data protection. Compliance-driven scanning can help identify and address potential violations before they lead to legal or regulatory consequences.

In summary, security considerations are paramount in cloud network scanning. As organizations increasingly rely on cloud services and infrastructure, they must adopt a security-first approach to scanning activities. This entails safeguarding data, optimizing resource usage, addressing false positives and negatives, coordinating with IDS/IPS solutions, using cloud-native tools, maintaining accurate asset inventories, and aligning with compliance standards. By prioritizing security in cloud network scanning, organizations can proactively identify and remediate vulnerabilities, ultimately enhancing the security of their cloud environments.

Chapter 7: Web Application Assessment with NMAP

Identifying web application vulnerabilities is a critical aspect of modern cybersecurity, as web applications have become a prime target for cyberattacks due to their ubiquity and potential for exposing sensitive data.

One common method for identifying web application vulnerabilities is through the use of automated scanning tools, such as Burp Suite, OWASP ZAP, or Acunetix. These tools can be run from the command line using the following syntax:

arduino

```
burp-cli -u http://example.com -a username:password -s scanner-config.xml -l scan-logs.txt
```

In this command, we specify the target URL with **-u**, provide authentication credentials with **-a**, specify a scanner configuration file with **-s**, and define a log file for scan results with **-l**. Running an automated scan can help identify common vulnerabilities like SQL injection, cross-site scripting (XSS), and insecure server configurations.

Additionally, manual testing plays a crucial role in identifying web application vulnerabilities. Security professionals can use command-line tools like cURL to send HTTP requests and analyze responses:

arduino

```
curl -X GET http://example.com/login
```

Here, we send a GET request to the login page of the web application. Manual testing allows for in-depth examination of input fields, request parameters, and response behaviors to uncover vulnerabilities that automated tools may miss.

One common web application vulnerability is SQL injection, which occurs when an attacker manipulates input data to execute arbitrary SQL queries on the database. To identify SQL injection vulnerabilities, testers can use tools like SQLMap from the command line:

bash

```
sqlmap -u http://example.com/login?username=test --data="username=test&password=password" --cookie="session=123456" --dbs
```

In this example, SQLMap is used to test a login page for SQL injection vulnerabilities. The **-u** flag specifies the target URL, **--data** provides POST data if applicable, **--cookie** includes session information, and **--dbs** requests a list of available databases.

Another critical web application vulnerability is cross-site scripting (XSS), which allows attackers to inject malicious scripts into web pages viewed by other users. To identify XSS vulnerabilities, testers can use command-line tools like XSSer:

bash

```
xsser -u http://example.com/search?q=test
```

In this command, XSSer is pointed to a search page with the **-u** flag, and it automatically scans for potential XSS vulnerabilities by injecting payloads into user input fields.

Web application scanners often generate detailed reports that provide information about identified vulnerabilities, their severity, and recommendations for remediation. These reports are valuable for both security professionals and developers tasked with fixing the issues.

In addition to automated scanning and manual testing, it's essential to keep web application components and libraries up to date. Outdated software components may contain known vulnerabilities that attackers can exploit. Developers should regularly check for updates and apply patches as needed.

Furthermore, security headers and best practices can help mitigate web application vulnerabilities. For instance, the HTTP Strict Transport Security (HSTS) header instructs web browsers to communicate with a site only over secure HTTPS connections, reducing the risk of man-in-the-middle attacks.

To deploy HSTS via the command line, the server's configuration file (e.g., Apache's httpd.conf or Nginx's nginx.conf) can be edited to include the following directives:

For Apache:

vbnet

```
Header always set Strict-Transport-Security "max-age=31536000; includeSubDomains; preload"
```

For Nginx:

vbnet

```
add_header Strict-Transport-Security "max-age=31536000; includeSubDomains; preload";
```

These commands set the HSTS header with a one-year maximum age and include subdomains. The "preload" directive indicates that the site should be included in browser preload lists, further enhancing security.

Cross-Origin Resource Sharing (CORS) headers can also be configured to control which domains are permitted to access resources on a web application. To set up CORS policies from the command line, the server's configuration can be adjusted accordingly.

For Apache:

arduino

```
Header always set Access-Control-Allow-Origin "https://trusted-domain.com"
```

For Nginx:

mathematica

add_header Access-Control-Allow-Origin "https://trusted-domain.com";

These commands specify that only the specified trusted domain is allowed to access resources on the web application.

Finally, implementing a Web Application Firewall (WAF) can provide an additional layer of protection against web application vulnerabilities. WAFs can be configured and managed through command-line interfaces, allowing security teams to define rules and policies for blocking malicious traffic.

s

```
waf-cli config --rule-set web-application-rules waf-cli rule
create --name "SQL Injection Protection" --action BLOCK --
match-type CONTAINS_SQL
```

In this example, the WAF is configured to use a rule set for web application protection, and a specific rule is created to block requests containing SQL injection patterns.

In summary, identifying web application vulnerabilities is crucial for maintaining the security of online services. Security professionals should employ a combination of automated scanning tools, manual testing, and best practices, such as keeping software components up to date, configuring security headers, and deploying Web Application Firewalls. By actively addressing vulnerabilities, organizations can protect their web applications from potential threats and breaches, ultimately ensuring the safety and trust of their users.

NMAP, often associated with network scanning, can also be a valuable tool for web application security testing. While it may not replace dedicated web application scanners, it can provide valuable insights and complement existing testing methodologies.

To leverage NMAP for web application security testing, it's important to understand its capabilities and limitations. NMAP primarily excels at network-level scanning and fingerprinting, which can help identify open ports, services, and potentially vulnerable server configurations.

One of the fundamental techniques when using NMAP for web application testing is to conduct port scanning. By determining which ports are open on a web server, you can identify potentially accessible services and gain insight into the server's architecture. The command to perform a basic port scan with NMAP looks like this:

```
nmap -p 80,443 example.com
```

In this command, NMAP scans ports 80 (HTTP) and 443 (HTTPS) on the example.com domain. It provides information about whether these ports are open, closed, or filtered, which is useful for understanding the server's configuration.

Beyond basic port scanning, NMAP offers scripts and additional options that can aid in web application security testing. One such script is the HTTP Enumeration script, which attempts to identify details about the web server and any running web applications. You can run it like this:

arduino

```
nmap --script http-enum example.com
```

This script may reveal the web server software, supported HTTP methods, and potentially interesting URLs. It helps in identifying the technology stack and potential vulnerabilities associated with the web application.

While NMAP can provide valuable information, it's essential to remember its limitations. NMAP's primary focus is on network scanning, not deep application-level testing. It won't discover vulnerabilities like Cross-Site Scripting (XSS) or SQL injection by itself. For these types of vulnerabilities, you'll need specialized web vulnerability scanners.

Moreover, NMAP is limited to the information that's publicly available without authentication. It won't uncover hidden pages or sensitive data that requires login credentials.

When using NMAP for web application security testing, it's crucial to follow ethical testing practices and obtain proper authorization. Scanning websites or web applications without permission can lead to legal consequences.

In some cases, NMAP can also be used to identify potential security misconfigurations on a web server. For example, it can check for the presence of open network services like FTP, Telnet, or SSH, which should ideally be restricted or disabled on web servers.

To scan for these services, you can use NMAP with specific port numbers:

```
nmap -p 21,22,23 example.com
```

This command scans for FTP, SSH, and Telnet services on the example.com domain. Identifying these open services can help administrators take appropriate security measures.

Another use case for NMAP in web application security testing is identifying open HTTP methods. For instance, some web servers might allow potentially dangerous HTTP methods like PUT or DELETE, which could lead to security vulnerabilities. NMAP can be employed to discover allowed methods:

```
nmap --script http-methods example.com
```

This script checks which HTTP methods are supported by the web server on example.com. If it finds methods like PUT or DELETE, it could indicate a security concern that should be addressed.

NMAP can also be used to perform a banner grab, which involves capturing information from the server's HTTP response headers. This information may include server software versions and technologies in use. While it's not a definitive security test, it can provide clues about the server's configuration:

nmap --script http-headers example .com

The HTTP Headers script checks for various headers and their values in the server's response. It can reveal details about the server's software and other configuration information.

Additionally, NMAP offers the HTTP PUT test script, which checks if the server allows HTTP PUT requests. This is significant because allowing PUT requests can pose security risks, as it permits users to upload files to the server:

arduino

nmap --script http-put example.com

The HTTP PUT test script can help identify whether the server permits file uploads via HTTP PUT requests.

In summary, while NMAP is not a replacement for specialized web application scanners, it can be a valuable addition to your web application security testing toolkit. NMAP's network scanning and scripting capabilities can help identify potential security misconfigurations, open services, and HTTP methods that may pose security risks. However, it should be used in conjunction with dedicated web vulnerability scanners and always in an ethical and authorized manner. Remember that web application security is a multifaceted discipline that requires a combination of tools and techniques to ensure comprehensive coverage and protection against potential threats.

Chapter 8: Red Team and Ethical Hacking with NMAP

In the world of cybersecurity, NMAP has earned its reputation as a versatile and powerful tool, often associated with network scanning and reconnaissance. However, its utility extends beyond the realm of defensive security practices, as it has also found a valuable place in the toolkit of red teamers and penetration testers. This chapter delves into the various ways in which NMAP can be effectively utilized in red team operations, offering a deeper understanding of its capabilities and the strategic advantages it brings to the table.

Red teaming is a cybersecurity practice that simulates real-world attacks on an organization's infrastructure, applications, and personnel. It helps organizations identify vulnerabilities, weaknesses, and areas for improvement in their security posture. While red teamers often employ a wide range of tools and techniques, NMAP's versatility makes it an indispensable asset in their arsenal.

One of the primary use cases for NMAP in red team operations is network mapping and reconnaissance. Red teamers leverage NMAP to gather information about the target network, including discovering live hosts, open ports, and services running on those ports. The command to perform a basic network scan with NMAP is as follows:

r

nmap -sn -T4 -F target_network

In this command, "-sn" specifies a ping scan to identify live hosts, "-T4" sets the timing template for faster execution, and "-F" scans the most common 100 ports. The result is a snapshot of the target network's footprint, providing valuable insights into its topology.

NMAP's scripting engine, known as the NMAP Scripting Engine (NSE), plays a pivotal role in red team operations. Red teamers can write custom NSE scripts or leverage existing ones to automate tasks, exploit vulnerabilities, or gather specific information from target systems. These scripts can be executed using the following command syntax:

nmap --script script_name target

For instance, red teamers can use NMAP to automate vulnerability scanning by running scripts that identify known vulnerabilities on target systems. This approach allows them to identify weaknesses that malicious actors might exploit and helps organizations prioritize patching efforts.

NMAP's scripting capabilities can also be harnessed for privilege escalation during red team operations. Custom NSE scripts can be developed to exploit vulnerabilities and gain elevated access to target systems. While this approach requires responsible and authorized testing, it demonstrates the importance of NMAP in assessing security measures from a red team perspective.

Stealth and evasion techniques are crucial in red teaming, as they aim to avoid detection while conducting reconnaissance and exploitation. NMAP offers various scan techniques that red teamers can utilize to remain covert during their operations. The "-sS" flag, for instance, performs a stealthy SYN scan that can help evade intrusion detection systems (IDS) and firewalls. This command initiates a SYN scan:

nmap -sS target

Another valuable aspect of NMAP for red teamers is its ability to perform version detection. Red teamers can use the "-sV" flag to identify specific software versions and services running on open ports. This information is invaluable for crafting tailored exploits and attacks, as it allows red teamers to target known vulnerabilities associated with particular software versions.

nmap -sV target

In addition to its active scanning capabilities, NMAP can also be employed passively in red team operations. Passive reconnaissance involves collecting information about a target network without directly interacting with it. Red teamers can use NMAP's passive operating system detection (-O) to gather data about the target network's systems and services based on network traffic analysis.

mathematica

nmap -O target

NMAP's versatility extends to post-exploitation activities in red team operations. After gaining access to a target system, red teamers can use NMAP to pivot within the network and conduct lateral movement. For example, they can perform internal scans to discover other vulnerable systems or assess the security posture of the internal network.

nmap -p- -T4 target_network

This command scans all ports within the target network using a timing template of T4. It helps red teamers identify potential entry points or weak links within the organization's internal infrastructure.

While NMAP is a powerful tool for red teamers, it is essential to emphasize the ethical and responsible use of this tool. Red team operations should always be conducted with proper authorization and within the boundaries defined by the engagement scope. Unauthorized or malicious use of NMAP can lead to legal consequences and damage to an organization's reputation.

In summary, NMAP's adaptability and extensive feature set make it an indispensable asset for red teamers and penetration testers. Its ability to perform network mapping, vulnerability assessment, stealthy scans, and post-exploitation activities provides valuable insights and advantages during red team operations. However, it is crucial for red teamers to approach their work with ethics, responsibility, and adherence to legal standards to ensure that their actions align with the goals of improving security and protecting organizations from real-world threats.

Ethical hacking, also known as white-hat hacking, involves the authorized and responsible exploration of computer systems, networks, and applications to identify vulnerabilities and weaknesses that could be exploited by malicious actors. Ethical hackers use their skills and tools like NMAP to proactively assess and secure an organization's digital assets. Next, we'll delve into the world of ethical hacking techniques with NMAP, exploring how this versatile tool can be harnessed to strengthen cybersecurity defenses.

One of the fundamental aspects of ethical hacking with NMAP is network reconnaissance, which encompasses activities aimed at gathering information about a target network without causing harm or disruption. Ethical hackers employ NMAP to perform network scans and discover live hosts, open ports, and services running on those ports within the target network. The following command is a typical example of a network discovery scan:

nmap -sn target_network

In this command, "-sn" instructs NMAP to perform a ping scan, which identifies live hosts without probing open ports. This initial step helps ethical hackers understand the network's scope and potential entry points.

Port scanning is another crucial technique in ethical hacking, allowing hackers to identify which ports on a target system are open, closed, or filtered. NMAP offers various scanning options to suit different scenarios. The following command demonstrates a SYN scan, a common technique used for stealthy port scanning:

nmap -sS target

In this command, "-sS" specifies a SYN scan, which sends SYN packets to the target's ports, aiming to establish connections without completing the handshake. This approach can help evade intrusion detection systems and firewalls.

Ethical hackers can also leverage NMAP for service detection, which involves identifying the specific services and their versions running on open ports. This information is crucial for assessing potential vulnerabilities and weaknesses. The following command combines service detection with version detection:

nmap -sV target

With the "-sV" flag, NMAP not only identifies open ports but also determines the service and its version, providing ethical hackers with valuable insights into the target system's software stack.

Vulnerability assessment is a cornerstone of ethical hacking, and NMAP can play a pivotal role in this process. Ethical hackers can use NMAP's scripting engine, the NMAP Scripting Engine (NSE), to run custom or pre-built scripts that scan for known vulnerabilities on target systems. For instance, they can employ NMAP to identify common vulnerabilities and exposures (CVEs) associated with specific software versions running on open ports.

```
nmap --script vuln target
```

In this command, "--script vuln" instructs NMAP to run scripts designed to detect vulnerabilities. Ethical hackers can use the results to prioritize remediation efforts and strengthen security measures.

In ethical hacking engagements, stealth and evasion techniques are essential to minimize the risk of detection by intrusion detection systems (IDS) or other security mechanisms. NMAP provides options for conducting scans covertly. For example, the following command combines a SYN scan with timing adjustments for a stealthy approach:

```
nmap -sS -T4 target
```

In this command, "-T4" sets the timing template to be more aggressive while still being cautious to avoid detection.

Beyond network reconnaissance and vulnerability assessment, ethical hackers often engage in post-exploitation activities to assess the extent of compromise within a target network. NMAP can assist in this phase by conducting internal scans to identify other vulnerable systems or assess the security posture of the internal network.

```
nmap -p- target_network
```

The "-p-" flag scans all ports within the target network, helping ethical hackers uncover potential entry points or weak links within the organization's internal infrastructure.

It's crucial to emphasize that ethical hacking is conducted with explicit authorization and within the boundaries defined by the engagement scope. Ethical hackers must adhere to a strict code of ethics and legal standards to ensure that their actions align with the goal of improving security and protecting organizations from real-world threats. Unauthorized or malicious hacking activities can lead to serious legal consequences and harm an organization's reputation.

In summary, NMAP is a versatile and powerful tool in the ethical hacker's toolkit, providing essential capabilities for network reconnaissance, vulnerability assessment, and post-exploitation activities. When used responsibly and within the confines of ethical hacking engagements, NMAP can help organizations identify and address security weaknesses, ultimately fortifying their defenses against cyber threats.

Chapter 9: Advanced NMAP Scripting for Exploitation

Exploitation is a critical phase in cybersecurity that involves leveraging vulnerabilities discovered during the reconnaissance and vulnerability assessment stages to gain unauthorized access or control over a target system or network. Next, we'll explore exploitation concepts with NMAP, focusing on how this versatile tool can be used to identify and potentially exploit vulnerabilities, as well as the ethical considerations and best practices associated with these activities.

Identifying vulnerabilities is a crucial step in the exploitation process, and NMAP provides several features that can aid ethical hackers in this endeavor. One such feature is the NMAP Scripting Engine (NSE), a powerful framework that allows the execution of custom scripts to automate tasks such as vulnerability identification. These scripts, often referred to as NSE scripts, can be written by ethical hackers or sourced from the extensive NMAP script library, which contains pre-built scripts for various purposes.

To demonstrate the use of NSE scripts for identifying vulnerabilities, consider the following scenario. An ethical hacker is tasked with assessing the security of a web application running on a target server. They can utilize NMAP and an NSE script specifically designed for web application scanning:

```
nmap -p 80 --script http-vuln-cve2017-5638.nse target_server
```

In this command, the "--script" option is used to specify the NSE script "http-vuln-cve2017-5638.nse," which checks for a specific vulnerability (CVE-2017-5638) associated with the

Apache Struts framework commonly used in web applications.

However, ethical hackers must exercise caution and adhere to ethical guidelines when conducting vulnerability scans and exploiting weaknesses. Unauthorized exploitation or causing harm to a target system without proper authorization can lead to legal consequences and damage an organization's reputation.

Ethical hacking engagements should always involve explicit permission from the organization or individual responsible for the target system. Additionally, ethical hackers must operate within the defined scope of the engagement, respecting the boundaries set by the organization and focusing solely on assessing the security posture without causing disruption or damage.

One ethical consideration is the responsible disclosure of vulnerabilities. When ethical hackers discover vulnerabilities during their assessments, they should follow a responsible disclosure process, which typically involves notifying the affected organization or vendor and providing them with details about the vulnerability. This allows the organization to take appropriate remediation actions to protect their systems and users.

Ethical hackers should also prioritize the principle of "do no harm" throughout their engagements. While the goal is to identify and help remediate vulnerabilities, it's essential to avoid actions that could negatively impact the availability, integrity, or confidentiality of the target system or network.

When conducting exploitation tests, ethical hackers should use caution and avoid causing unintended consequences. For example, a vulnerability exploitation attempt may lead to system crashes, data loss, or unintended service disruptions. Therefore, thorough planning and risk assessment are essential before attempting any exploitation.

In ethical hacking engagements, a common approach is to simulate attacks and demonstrate the potential impact of vulnerabilities to the organization's stakeholders. This can include exploiting vulnerabilities in a controlled environment to show the consequences of a successful attack. Ethical hackers should document their findings meticulously, including the steps taken, the vulnerabilities exploited, and the potential impact.

Additionally, ethical hackers should provide recommendations and guidance on remediation measures. These recommendations may include patching or updating software, reconfiguring security settings, or implementing additional security controls to mitigate the identified vulnerabilities.

It's crucial to remember that ethical hacking is a collaborative effort between the ethical hacker and the organization being assessed. Communication and transparency are key elements of a successful engagement. Ethical hackers should maintain open channels of communication with the organization's security team and management, sharing findings and insights to support security improvement efforts.

In summary, exploitation concepts with NMAP involve the responsible identification and demonstration of vulnerabilities in target systems or networks. Ethical hackers use NMAP's capabilities, including the NSE scripting engine, to automate vulnerability identification and assess the potential impact of weaknesses. However, ethical considerations, legal compliance, and adherence to ethical hacking guidelines are paramount throughout the entire process to ensure the safety and security of all parties involved.

NSE (NMAP Scripting Engine) scripting is a powerful feature

of NMAP that goes beyond vulnerability identification and reconnaissance, allowing ethical hackers to actively exploit vulnerabilities when given explicit authorization. Next, we delve into the realm of NSE scripting for active exploits, exploring how these scripts can be used to simulate attacks, assess the impact of vulnerabilities, and provide valuable insights to organizations seeking to bolster their security defenses.

Active exploitation using NSE scripts is a controlled and ethical practice that aims to demonstrate the potential consequences of unaddressed vulnerabilities. Ethical hackers utilize NMAP's NSE capabilities to conduct controlled attacks within predefined boundaries, ensuring that the testing environment and the target systems are isolated from the production network to prevent any unintended disruptions.

To illustrate the concept of NSE scripting for active exploits, let's consider an example scenario. An ethical hacker has been granted permission to assess the security of a web application hosted on a target server. The web application is known to have a vulnerability in its authentication mechanism that allows for potential unauthorized access. The ethical hacker can leverage an NSE script designed for this purpose:

bash

```
nmap -p 80 --script http-brute --script-args http-brute.path="/login",http-brute.hostname="target_server" target_server
```

In this command, the NSE script "http-brute" is employed to conduct a brute-force attack against the web application's login page on port 80. The script takes additional arguments, specifying the login path and the target server's hostname. The purpose here is not to compromise the system but to demonstrate the risk associated with weak authentication mechanisms.

Ethical hackers should always operate within a well-defined scope and adhere to strict rules of engagement, which include obtaining explicit authorization from the organization or individual responsible for the target systems. Additionally, the scope should clearly specify the limitations and boundaries of the testing, ensuring that only authorized systems and vulnerabilities are assessed.

A critical aspect of NSE scripting for active exploits is the careful selection of scripts and the consideration of potential impacts. Ethical hackers must choose scripts that align with the objectives of the engagement and prioritize those that simulate real-world attack scenarios while minimizing risks. Risk assessment and planning play a significant role in ensuring the safety and security of the testing environment and target systems.

During active exploitation tests, ethical hackers must be vigilant and prepared to halt any actions that may lead to unintended consequences. For example, a script simulating a denial-of-service (DoS) attack could inadvertently disrupt a target system's availability. Monitoring and aborting scripts if necessary is essential to prevent harm and maintain control.

Documentation is paramount in active exploitation testing. Ethical hackers must meticulously record their actions, including the scripts used, the vulnerabilities exploited, and the outcomes observed. This documentation serves as a crucial reference for reporting findings and providing organizations with a clear understanding of the risks associated with unpatched vulnerabilities.

Reporting findings is a fundamental aspect of ethical hacking engagements involving active exploits. Ethical hackers should prepare detailed reports that not only highlight the vulnerabilities but also describe the potential impact, including any sensitive data that could be compromised or systems that could be disrupted. Recommendations for remediation should be provided to assist organizations in addressing identified weaknesses.

A responsible disclosure process is essential when active exploits reveal critical vulnerabilities. Ethical hackers should follow a structured procedure for notifying the affected organization or vendor of the vulnerabilities and their potential impact. This allows the organization to take prompt remediation actions to mitigate the risks.

Ethical hackers should maintain clear and open communication with the organization's stakeholders, including the security team and management. Transparency and collaboration are essential to ensure that security improvements are implemented effectively and that any concerns or questions are addressed promptly.

In summary, NSE scripting for active exploits is a valuable tool in the ethical hacker's arsenal, enabling them to simulate attacks, assess vulnerabilities, and provide organizations with insights to enhance their security defenses. However, this practice must always be conducted within a well-defined scope, with explicit authorization, and with careful consideration of potential impacts. Ethical hackers play a crucial role in identifying and mitigating security risks, and responsible testing is essential to the safety and security of all parties involved.

Chapter 10: Beyond NMAP: Integrating Other Tools and Resources

NMAP, as a versatile and comprehensive network scanning tool, plays a vital role in the field of cybersecurity, but it is rarely used in isolation. To understand its significance, it's essential to consider NMAP in the context of other security tools and how it complements and integrates with them.

In today's complex cybersecurity landscape, organizations rely on a wide array of security tools and technologies to protect their networks and data. These tools include intrusion detection systems (IDS), intrusion prevention systems (IPS), firewalls, antivirus software, vulnerability scanners, and more. NMAP, with its capabilities for network discovery, scanning, and vulnerability assessment, often serves as a foundational component of these broader security ecosystems.

One of NMAP's primary functions is network mapping and reconnaissance, providing organizations with a clear understanding of their network's layout and potential vulnerabilities. This information is invaluable for network administrators and security professionals who need to ensure that only authorized devices are connected to the network and that security policies are effectively enforced.

In the context of an IDS and IPS, NMAP's role becomes even more critical. These systems are designed to detect and prevent malicious activities within a network. NMAP can be used to simulate various network scans and attacks, allowing organizations to test the effectiveness of their IDS/IPS configurations. By using NMAP to emulate real-world threats, security teams can fine-tune their detection and prevention rules, ensuring that the systems are capable of identifying and blocking malicious behavior. Additionally, NMAP can assist in tuning firewalls and access control lists (ACLs) by simulating network traffic and helping organizations identify potential gaps in their security policies. By running NMAP scans against their own infrastructure, organizations can determine whether their firewalls are effectively filtering unwanted traffic and blocking unauthorized access attempts.

NMAP also integrates seamlessly with vulnerability scanning tools, such as Nessus or OpenVAS. These tools are designed to identify known vulnerabilities in network services and applications. NMAP's scripting engine allows users to develop custom scripts that can be executed alongside vulnerability scans, enhancing the depth and accuracy of vulnerability assessments.

Moreover, NMAP's scripting capabilities extend its utility beyond traditional network scanning. For example, NMAP scripts can interact with web applications, attempting to exploit known vulnerabilities or discover misconfigurations. This approach is particularly useful in web application security testing, where NMAP can be used alongside specialized web application security scanners to provide a comprehensive assessment of an organization's online assets.

When considering endpoint security, NMAP can assist in identifying open ports and services on individual devices. This information can be valuable for security administrators tasked with ensuring that endpoints are adequately protected and that unnecessary services are disabled or patched.

Intrusion detection and prevention tools often benefit from NMAP's ability to conduct stealthy and evasive scans. These scans are designed to mimic the behavior of sophisticated attackers who attempt to avoid detection. By using NMAP to test the effectiveness of their detection mechanisms, organizations can better prepare for real-world threats.

Another area where NMAP shines is in its integration with security information and event management (SIEM) systems. SIEM platforms aggregate and analyze security data from various sources, including network traffic, logs, and alerts. NMAP can feed valuable network information into SIEM systems, enriching the data available for correlation and analysis. This integration enhances an organization's ability to detect and respond to security incidents.

Beyond traditional network security, NMAP has also found utility in the realm of cloud security. As organizations migrate their resources to cloud environments, NMAP can be adapted to scan cloud infrastructure for vulnerabilities, misconfigurations, and exposure to security risks. This ensures that security considerations are not overlooked when transitioning to the cloud.

In summary, NMAP's role in the context of other security tools is that of a versatile and essential component. It enhances the capabilities of intrusion detection, prevention systems, firewalls, vulnerability scanners, and more. NMAP's adaptability, scripting engine, and comprehensive network scanning capabilities make it a valuable asset in today's dynamic and ever-evolving cybersecurity landscape. By integrating NMAP into their security toolsets, organizations can bolster their defenses, improve incident response, and stay one step ahead of emerging threats.

As you delve deeper into the world of network security and the extensive capabilities of NMAP, it becomes evident that a comprehensive approach to security requires an expanded arsenal of tools and techniques. While NMAP is a powerful and versatile tool, it should not be the sole instrument in your security toolkit. Instead, it should be complemented by a variety of other tools and strategies to ensure comprehensive security coverage for your network.

One critical aspect of comprehensive security is the need for continuous monitoring and assessment of your network's health and security posture. NMAP excels at providing periodic snapshots of your network's status, but it's equally important to have tools that offer real-time monitoring and alerting capabilities. Intrusion detection systems (IDS) and intrusion prevention systems (IPS) are crucial components in this regard.

These systems monitor network traffic in real-time, looking for patterns and behaviors that may indicate malicious activity. When a potential threat is detected, they can trigger alerts or take automated actions to mitigate the risk. Popular open-source IDS/IPS solutions include Snort and Suricata, which can be deployed alongside NMAP to create a robust security monitoring infrastructure.

In addition to real-time monitoring, vulnerability management tools are essential for identifying and addressing security weaknesses in your network. While NMAP can help identify open ports and services, dedicated vulnerability scanners go a step further by pinpointing known vulnerabilities in those services. Tools like Nessus, OpenVAS, and Qualys are commonly used in this capacity.

To ensure that vulnerabilities are promptly addressed, it's essential to integrate your vulnerability management tools with a robust patch management system. This system can automate the process of deploying patches and updates to vulnerable systems, reducing the window of opportunity for attackers. For Windows environments, Microsoft's WSUS (Windows Server Update Services) is a commonly used solution, while Linux systems often leverage tools like Red Hat Satellite or Spacewalk.

Another facet of comprehensive security is the protection of sensitive data and communication. Encryption plays a pivotal role in safeguarding data as it travels over networks. Tools such as OpenSSL and Let's Encrypt provide the means to implement strong encryption for data in transit, securing sensitive information from eavesdropping and interception.

While NMAP is primarily focused on network reconnaissance and vulnerability assessment, a comprehensive security strategy must also encompass endpoint security. Endpoint protection platforms (EPP) and endpoint detection and response (EDR) solutions are crucial for safeguarding individual devices, such as laptops and servers. Leading EPP solutions include Symantec Endpoint Protection, McAfee Endpoint Security, and CrowdStrike Falcon.

For organizations embracing cloud computing, cloud security tools and practices are indispensable. Cloud security posture management (CSPM) solutions, like Palo Alto Networks Prisma Cloud and AWS Security Hub, help organizations identify and rectify misconfigurations and security risks in their cloud environments. NMAP can be adapted to scan cloud infrastructure, but CSPM tools offer specialized capabilities tailored to the unique challenges of cloud security.

Security information and event management (SIEM) systems are vital for aggregating and analyzing security data from various sources across your network. They provide valuable insights into security incidents and trends, enabling security teams to detect and respond to threats effectively. Popular SIEM solutions include Splunk, IBM QRadar, and Elastic SIEM (formerly known as ELK Stack).

In the realm of threat intelligence, organizations can benefit from threat intelligence platforms (TIPs) and feeds. These resources provide valuable information about emerging threats, indicators of compromise (IOCs), and attack trends. TIPs like ThreatConnect and Anomali help organizations make informed decisions about their security posture and adapt their defenses accordingly.

For organizations with a red teaming or penetration testing focus, tools like Metasploit and Cobalt Strike provide advanced capabilities for simulating cyberattacks and assessing an organization's resilience to threats. These tools can be integrated with NMAP to execute complex attacks and identify vulnerabilities that may be exploitable by real adversaries.

Finally, incident response tools are crucial for efficiently managing and mitigating security incidents when they occur. Solutions like TheHive and MISP (Malware Information Sharing Platform & Threat Sharing) facilitate collaboration among incident response teams, ensuring that incidents are contained and resolved promptly.

In summary, while NMAP is a cornerstone tool in the realm of network scanning and security assessment, it is but one piece of the larger puzzle of comprehensive security. To truly protect your network and data, it's essential to expand your arsenal with a diverse range of tools and strategies. From real-time monitoring with IDS/IPS to vulnerability management, encryption, endpoint protection, and cloud security, a holistic approach to security encompasses a multitude of tools and practices. By carefully selecting and integrating these tools into your security posture, you can build a robust defense against an ever-evolving threat landscape.

Conclusion

In the ever-evolving landscape of cybersecurity, knowledge and expertise in network scanning and security are essential for organizations and individuals alike. The "NMAP Network Scanning Series" and the "Network Security, Monitoring, and Scanning Library" provide a comprehensive and invaluable resource for those seeking to enhance their skills, protect their networks, and gain mastery in the art of network reconnaissance.

Throughout this four-book bundle, we have embarked on a journey that begins with the fundamentals and gradually leads to advanced techniques and strategies. "Book 1: NMAP for Beginners" serves as the foundational stepping stone, introducing readers to the basics of network scanning and guiding them through practical exercises.

As we progress into "Book 2: NMAP Mastery," the series delves deeper into the world of network analysis. Readers are exposed to advanced scanning methods, scripting, and customizations, empowering them to conduct in-depth assessments and gain a deeper understanding of network vulnerabilities.

"Book 3: NMAP Security Essentials" reinforces the importance of network protection by imparting expert skills to secure and defend against potential threats. It provides insights into securing open ports, services, and hardening network devices to maintain the integrity and confidentiality of data.

Finally, in "Book 4: NMAP Beyond Boundaries," we venture into the realm of complex network reconnaissance, including geospatial mapping, IoT security, cloud scanning, and web application assessment. The series concludes by equipping readers with the knowledge and tools to tackle even the most intricate network challenges.

The "NMAP Network Scanning Series" and the "Network Security, Monitoring, and Scanning Library" represent a holistic approach to network security. They empower readers to adopt a proactive stance in safeguarding their networks against potential threats and vulnerabilities. With the skills and insights gained from these books, individuals and organizations can fortify their defenses, maintain compliance, and ensure the integrity of their network infrastructure.

In an era where cybersecurity is of paramount importance, the knowledge and expertise presented in this series are invaluable. We hope that readers find these books not only informative but also transformative, enabling them to navigate the ever-changing landscape of network security with confidence and competence.

Thank you for embarking on this journey of learning and mastery with us. May the insights and skills gained from the "NMAP Network Scanning Series" and the "Network Security, Monitoring, and Scanning Library" serve as powerful tools in your ongoing quest for network security excellence.